SCENES FROM THE PAST : 16 (PAR

THE MIDLAND ROUTE
MANCHESTER
—— PART ONE ——
CENTRAL to NEW MILLS
Via DIDSBURY, STOCKPORT & MARPLE

E. M. JOHNSON

New Mills South Junction c.1920: New Mills South Junction was where the New Mills and Heaton Mersey line, fully operational from 1902 onwards, met the "old" line via Stockport Tiviot Dale and Romiley. Thus was made the Midland Railway's last thrust towards Manchester; a great company's overture to the twentieth century. What more appropriate introduction could there be to this location, with its connotation of easy, high-speed running, than this view of a Johnson "Single" gliding effortlessly along? No.**633** with its three clerestory coaches has come along the "new" line, has cleared the junction and is proceeding along the Up Fast line towards Bugsworth. Off to the right is the "old" line from Romiley via New Mills Central; these tracks form Down and Up Slow respectively between here and Bugsworth. Standing out against the sky and the picturesque backdrop of hills is a splendid array of Midland semaphores-the splitting arms relate to the crossings from "new" to "old" lines and vice-versa with repeating lower arms; the Distants are for New Mills Goods box. Notice, too, the vertical white stripe still set on a red ground for the Distants; yellow with black fishtails and yellow/orange spectacles was some years off yet.
Cowan collection, National Railway Museum

Contents ...

Manchester Central, June 10th. 1953: 1.32 in the afternoon shows the magnificent station frontage decorated for the festivities of the Coronation of H.M. Queen Elizabeth II on the Tuesday of the previous week. The authorities have even managed to fly the Union Flag on top of the 90 ft. high roof! Worth another look are the now almost vintage motor vehicles-Austin, Humber, Jaguar, Standard and Ford are some of the makes on parade. Notice the belted raincoats and Trilby hat sported by the various figures, almost anachronistic items in today's fashion wardrobe. The wooden booking offices mentioned in the Introduction can be clearly seen under the front canopy.

G.K.Fox collection

Foreword

This book had its origins in the wake of my "Railways in and around the Manchester Suburbs." Just after publication, in January 1990, I mounted a small exhibition in Didsbury Library to show something of the railway that passed through the village. This was enthusiastically received and Greg Fox made the suggestion that, maybe, I could work some of the Didsbury material into a broader whole showing the Manchester South District Railway from the erstwhile Manchester Central station through South Manchester and Stockport as far as Chinley.

The resulting work is presented here and let me say that there has been nothing so far which has given me more pleasure to write. I first watched trains on this line at around the tender age of four years. Through my school and teenage life it was always "The Didsbury Line" that held the greatest fascination; even after trips to the mighty Crewe, it was back to Withington, Didsbury and Parr's Wood that we came for our thrills-formative years indeed! Well-remembered are the days of school holidays stood on the bridge that connected Didsbury Park with School Lane. In 1959, the year I left school, West Didsbury Station seemed to hold a special fascination for me. Days spent doing nothing more than just watching the trains pass by, at the expense, it has to be added, of GCE O-Level revision!

The 1960s opened with the introduction of "The Midland Pullman." We didn't realise it then, but that decade was to be the line's last. An Indian Summer had begun which would last until 1966. Less than three years later, by the end of 1969, the section from Chorlton Junction to Cheadle Heath, the railway of my childhood, would be no more.

Towards the end of the production of the manuscript's first draft, it was decided to split the work into two rough halves. This, the first part, covers the "old" 1880 route from Manchester Central via Chorlton-cum-Hardy and Didsbury, through Stockport and Marple as far as New Mills South Junction. A second volume will take the story on from Cheadle Heath via Disley Tunnel-the "new" line of 1902-to New Mills South Junction and, finally, Chinley.

E.M.Johnson,
Burnage, Manchester.

Dedication

With this book, I would like to remember my dear friend from childhood, Richard Cherrington. It was with Richard that I spent so many happy times doing nothing better than watching trains at Didsbury, Heaton Mersey and Cheadle Heath. What fun we had.

South of Didsbury, May 25th. 1953: This fine and sunny Whit Monday would have seen excursions travelling all over the British Railways network. The Manchester South District line was no exception and here, viewed from the overbridge between School Lane and Parr's Wood Road, is Stanier 2-6-4 tank No. **42469** ambling along with a Manchester Central to Matlock excursion. Examples of excursion fares for the 1950s show (in 1957) Manchester to Matlock for 9/3d, an extra 3d. (!) took passengers on to Matlock Bath, Chinley 3/4d, Edale 4/6d, and Sheffield 8/9d. The keen-eyed may notice that the track has been re-ballasted, an almost white line of limestone stretches into the distance as far as the eye can see. The tall, double-armed home signal was a familiar sight here until May 1958. Across by Didsbury Park can be seen the well-tended allotments providing a grandstand view of this splendid main line. Now, only the slender Poplar trees survive to grace the background; almost the whole of the area bounded by the railway was acquired by the Post Office in August, 1979. Today, the all-pervading silver of the British Telecom vehicles that have made their home here are the dominant force amongst the dereliction that once was the railway.
B.K.B.Green

THE MIDLAND ROUTE FROM MANCHESTER
———— PART ONE ————
CENTRAL to NEW MILLS

Manchester to London
A Complex History of Rivalries

The term "Market Share," a phrase beloved of the present-day business fraternity, though it may well be recently coined, describes a phenomenom as old, surely, as the principles and practice of trading and markets themselves. As students of railway history we commit ourselves, maybe unwittingly, to the study of such things. Politicking and machination were the stuff of the 19th century railway scene, a ferment of industrial super-power and ruthless, dogged empire building. Standing astride this scene, colossus-like, were the figures of such people as Sir Edward Watkin, Sir Richard Moon, Richard Shipley Ellis and Sir James Allport. Power, as is ever the case where human endeavour is thrust, was at the heart of their struggle. Power to buy up land, lay down railways and earn rich dividends from the mass movement of freight and people.

In an endeavour to capture for itself a slice of the lucrative London-Manchester rail-borne traffic, that bold and thrusting Victorian enterprise known as the Midland Railway had, via various agreements, secured a foothold in the joint tenure of Manchester's London Road station with the Manchester, Sheffield & Lincolnshire company.

A rail journey from Manchester to London's Euston Square, travelling via Warrington and Birmingham on the Grand Junction Railway, had been possible from as early as September 1838. The GJR, along with the Manchester and Birmingham Railway were fused to form the LNWR in 1846. This marriage thwarted the proposed route of the Manchester, Buxton, Matlock and Midlands Junction Railway (MBM&MJR) from Ambergate on the North Midland line north-westwards to Lancashire. Passing through Matlock, Bakewell and Buxton, the railway would have joined the Manchester and Birmingham company's line at Cheadle. In the event, this proposal became barren and the line finished up as an 11½ mile branch from Ambergate to Rowsley, opening on June 4th. 1849.

The MBM&MJR had been incorporated, along with the North Midland company, the Midland Counties Railway, and the Birmingham and Derby Railway to form the Midland Railway in 1844. On June 1st. 1852 the MBM&MJR was leased to the Midland and the London & North-Western companies. Unfortunately for the Midland, the LNWR pulled the rug from under it by its involvement in the Stockport, Disley and Whaley Bridge Railway (SD&WB) who had ideas of building a line from Stockport to Buxton. This line opened to Furness Vale on June 9th. 1857. An extension reached the Roman spa town on June 15th. 1863. Three years later, on November 16th. 1866, the SD&WBR was absorbed into the LNWR. However, the Midland, as ever, had been busy. Just two weeks before the London and North Western opened their station in Buxton, the Midland's branch northwards-the Rowsley and Buxton Extension-was opened, to arrive side by side in the town-the two stone facades standing to rub shoulders until modern times. Even at this relatively early juncture though, the Midland were not contemplating running through Buxton on a north-bound route from Derby. To complete the picture of the Midland's first entry into Manchester, it is necessary to re-trace our steps to March 1858 when the Manchester, Sheffield and Lincolnshire Railway, that most unfairly maligned of Victorian companies, opened a branch to Hyde off its Manchester-Sheffield main line. This by itself was not significant, but later that year an extension to Marple was authorised in the form of the Marple, New Mills and Hayfield Junction Railway.

F.S.Williams, in his celebrated treatise on the Midland Railway, recalls how, in the autumn of 1861, the company's chairman, Mr.Beale, the deputy chairman, Mr. Hutchinson, along with the legendary Mr.Allport, were visiting the Derbyshire countryside assessing the possibility of a Midland line northwards to Manchester. By chance, in a side lane, the party came across Mr.Lees, one of the M.S.& L's directors and two officers of the company who were out driving in a dog cart. The parties spent the day together and the outcome became part of railway history: the Midland were given access over M.S.& L. tracks "to Manchester, and every other place in Manchester, in Lancashire, or Cheshire, or beyond." Doubtless, the agreement had been enhanced by the fact that Allport had spent nearly four years as general manager of the Sheffield company.

From this remarkable encounter, then, had sprung an agreement enabling the Midland to extend their line from a point eastwards of Buxton, at Miller's Dale, north-westwards through the Derbyshire hills, via Peak Forest, Chapel-en-le-Frith and Chinley to join the MS&L at New Mills, to where the latter had arrived on July 1st. 1865. Sir Edward Watkin, the M.S.& L's mercurial chairman, is said never to have forgiven his board for arranging the terms of the agreement, which he thought strongly favoured the Midland, while he was abroad in the U.S.A.

The Midland had had a tough time in their assault on the North-West. Going north from Miller's Dale, the line reached 985 feet above sea -level, while just beyond this point, Dove Holes Tunnel, 1 mile, 1,224 yards had been driven-a tortuous process taking more than three years to complete, involving the loss of human life, attended by flooding and roof collapse as various underground water springs were penetrated.

The line to new Mills was opened for passenger traffic in February, 1867. The previous year, in the autumn of 1866, following an exceptionally wet season, no less than sixteen acres of land slipped at Bugsworth, a hamlet just north of Chapel-en-le-Frith, taking away a five-arched viaduct. To rectify this catastrophe the Midland employed all the Victorian muscle it could lay hands on. For about ten weeks more than four hundred men toiled night and day-building a new timber viaduct, which Williams records as having used about 50,000 feet of Baltic timber, making two skew bridges of 30 foot span with wrought iron girders, and provided an embankment at one end of the line and a rock cutting at the other.

Manchester's London Road station thus became the focus for Midland traffic from London, rubbing shoulders with that of the LNWR. London Road was jointly administered by the Sheffield and North-Western companies under the terms of the London Road Station Act of 1859. Interestingly, the Midland trains entering London Road in these early days had originated from King's Cross, St.Pancras not being opened until October 1st. 1868. London Road itself must have been an incredible place in those days; Williams records that no less than 450 trains used its platforms in a 24-hour period. With predictable tenacity the Midland had consolidated its position in the north's cotton capital by building a large goods station within a stone's throw of London Road in the Ancoats district on land previously occupied by Ancoats Hall. Ancoats Goods opened for traffic on May 2nd. 1870. In the mid-nineteenth century this city-centre district was alive with all sorts of manufacturing industry, the warehouse itself being a very short distance from Manchester's main produce markets at Smithfield, near Oldham Road. The establishment of such a large goods complex within spitting distance of its main rival was something of a coup.

Reference to a railway map of Manchester will show the somewhat circuitous route that Midland trains took using M.S.&.L tracks from New Mills via Romiley into their new-found terminus. Not that this was to last for long. On July 16th. 1866 the Manchester and Stockport Railway Act, promoted by the M.S.&.L, had been passed. Providing 4½ miles of railway from Ashburys to Brinnington Junction on the Stockport and Woodley Junction line, together with a 2¾ mile branch to Romiley, the Midland now had an altogether better route to the north-west cotton capital. The new line had stations at Bredbury, Reddish and Belle Vue and was brought into use for passenger traffic on August 2nd. 1875.

Long before Sir Edward Watkin's dream of an independent line to the Capital became a reality, the Manchester, Sheffield and Lincolnshire Railway had formed an alliance with the Great Northern Company to run passenger services from Manchester to London King's Cross via Sheffield and Retford. This partnership was a fairly long-lived one, having begun on August 1st. 1857, it lasted right up until March 1899. Co-incidentally it was on the 15th. of that month that the Great Central's new London Extension from Annesley to Marylebone was opened for passenger traffic, yet another player in the London to Manchester game had arrived at the table.

Long-standing though the GN/MS&L alliance had been, its Sheffield route was long, and journey times, though speeded up to a reasonable 4¼ hours from 1884, were not competitive with those offered by the LNWR. Competition between the LNW and the MSL was, to say the least, fierce and, at times positively bellicose. The story of the North Western arresting passengers who had had the temerity to travel into London Road via Sheffield has passed into railway folklore but is, nevertheless, true.

To return to the Midland Railway and their determination to reach Manchester. As far back as 1864 the MS&L had expressed an interest in the Manchester and Cheadle Railway. Little appears to have been written down about this fascinating line and some details are worth recording. Parliamentary plans dated November 1864 with Sacre's name attached show a line of 5 miles, 8½ chains running south of Old Trafford, through Chorlton-cum-Hardy and over the brook by Hough End at the back of the Workhouse cemetery. The alignment continued past the back of Lumb Farm and skirted the River Mersey at Ford Bank, near to St.James' Parish church, Didsbury. The Mersey was then crossed and the line formed a junction at Heaton Mersey with the Stockport, Timperley and Altrincham Junction Railway.

This abortive line was re-projected in 1873 as The Manchester South District Railway and was spawned with the intention of reaching Alderley, a village in north Cheshire on the already authorised Macclesfield, Knutsford and Warrington Railway. Under this 1873 scheme the line would have begun at Throstle Nest Junction on the C.L.C. Cornbrook to Cressington line (which had then not been constructed).

A year later, in 1874, another Act, dated June 30th., offered a variation on the previous scheme. This time a junction with the original line to Alderley was proposed at a point mid-way between Withington and Didsbury, two southerly suburbs of Manchester. From here the line would run to Heaton Mersey to join the Cheshire Lines Railway. The Act of 1874 also provided for a further deviation from the original plan. This would have left the projected alignment near the river Bollin and joined up with the Macclesfield and Knutsford line nearer to Alderley village, then a hamlet with a population of around 1,000 souls.

Plans began to form into reality with the triumvirate that formed the C.L.C. (the G.N., the M.S.&.L and the Midland) considering the acquisition of the Manchester South District line. The Great Northern, however, were seemingly not interested. A subsequent offer was, also, turned down by the G.N. company. On hearing of this disagreement the Sheffield and Midland Committee expressed an interest in "such portions of the (South District) line as might be mutually agreed upon." Snags reared up when, in July 1876, as the Bill was passing through Parliament, Sir Edward Watkin expressed his reservations to the S & M and hinted that the Midland might prefer to tackle the undertaking themselves.

A further turn of events came about in January 1876 when the M.S.&.L gave the Midland three years notice to quit their side of London Road station. Traffic at London Road had been growing apace and the approach lines were severely congested. Thus spurned, the Midland were faced with little alternative but to look to the South District line. The Bill authorising construction of the line-Midland Railway (further powers Act) received the Royal Assent in August 1876. The South District Railway was to be vested in the Sheffield and Midland Committee with a provision for the Great Northern to become a partner. It was deemed that, should this arise, the powers under the Act would be transferred to C.L.C. ownership.

This period was one of intense activity on the Midland. May 1st. 1876 saw the opening of the famed Settle and Carlisle line giving the company its long-awaited independent access to Scottish traffic. In the Autumn of 1876 Sir Edward Watkin wrote to Edward Shipley Ellis, the Midland Chairman, stating that, if the Midland required a prompt answer to the ownership of the South District undertaking, then the M.S.&.L would insist on pulling out; at the same time Watkin requested an option for a further year. Ellis, for the Midland, replied: "It is an important object with us to proceed with the construction of part, at least, of the line as early as practicable and I presume you will not object to our exercising the powers of the Joint Committee in their name, pending the transfer of the line to ourselves, after giving you an idemnity."

Acting quickly, the Midland obtained parliamentary sanction in the form of the Midland Railway (Further Powers) Act dated 12th. July 1877. Under this Act, the powers of the South District line, hitherto vested in the Sheffield and Midland Committee, were transferred retrospectively (from August 11th. 1876) to the Midland company. Provision was also allowed for the Great Northern to become joint owners of the line, an option extended up until August 11th. 1878, but one which was never taken up.

Thus equipped, the mighty Midland were to finally gain their own route into Manchester. The South District scheme was to comprise two parts: firstly, the 1873 section from the quaintly-named Throstle Nest Junction on the new line to Liverpool as far as Didsbury, and, secondly, the section from the latter place to Heaton Mersey where a junction was formed with what ultimately became the C.L.C. Stockport to Glazebrook (hitherto the Stockport, Timperley and Altrincham Junction Railway) line which had opened to Deansgate Junction, Timperley, on the M.S.J.&A on December 1st. 1865 and had been mooted in the Manchester & Cheadle scheme of 1864.

Here we should pause to consider more fully the position and the geography at the Manchester end of the line. Prior to 1873 the C.L.C. trains between Manchester and Liverpool used running powers over the L.N.W.R. between Garston and Timperley Junction and thence traversed the lines of the M.S.J & A. into London Road. Sir Edward Watkin, the M.S.& L. Chairman, put forward a Bill (the M.S.& L. Railway Extension to Liverpool) for a new route to the port. The line comprised two parts: firstly, a railway from Old Trafford to Cressington to join the Garston and Liverpool Railway. Secondly, a line was to be built from Glazebrook, on the previous line, to form a junction with the Stockport, Timperley and Altrincham Junction Railway at Skelton West Junction, Altrincham. Under an Act of 1866 the junction with the M.S.J & A. was made at Cornbrook, the lines eventually opened for traffic in 1873.

The Midland Railway had joined the Cheshire Lines partnership in July, 1866. The power of the conglomerate had been strengthened in 1866 with the Cheshire Lines Act which gave over the ownership of the Godley and Woodley line, opened that year, and also the ownership of the Chester and West Cheshire Junction Railway.

But still, London Road was at the focus of things at the Manchester end of the line. Much capital expenditure had been undertaken in Liverpool with the building of the new Central Station and the construction of some 23 acres of dock complex at Huskisson. Under the Cheshire Lines Act of June 1872 powers were sought to build a central station in Manchester along with a 1 mile, 20 chain connecting line from Cornbrook. Opened on July 9th. 1877, the new Central station was sited on Windmill Street at the back of the Free Trade Hall and the Theatre Royal. Central Manchester in those days was a vastly different place from the mass of offices and shops that occupy the town centre today. Row upon row of sub-standard back-to-back houses occupied numerous streets, courts and alleys. Here, thousands of poor souls lived under the most wretched conditions; scarcely conceivable today and graphically described in the writings of Frederick Engels. From those poor hovels the populace would certainly have walked to work, maybe in of the metal foundries-a copper and bronze works was cleared to make way for the station-or one of the numerous cotton warehouses abounding in this, at that time the cotton capital of Great Britain.

The original Central station was to last less than three years, before the later structure, with its majestic single span mimicking St.Pancras supplanted it. This early station then became part of a goods depot surrounded, later on, by a complex of warehouses fronting onto Watson Street then, too, the site of a vast stock of indifferent housing. The new Central Station housed six platforms under the 210 feet wide roof reaching to a maximum height of 90 feet.

The first meeting of the Manchester South District Committee was held at Derby on October 31st. 1876. John.S.Wilkinson, the line's first engineer, was instructed to put plans in hand and draw up specifications and bills of quantity for the letting of tenders. Messrs. Mc.Gregor and Badman of Darwen, Lancashire, won the contract for construction of the line proper, which excluded buildings. Some idea of the tremendous fall in the value of money can be gleaned by noting the tender price of £145,790.13.11½d for the construction of just under 8 miles of main line double track railway. Costs, of course, are relative but it is worth recording that, today, preserved railways have to pay around £200 for one length of rail. Mc.Gregor and Badman also won the contract to build the South District's four stations: Chorlton-cum-Hardy, Withington, Didsbury and Heaton Mersey. The whole amounting to the seemingly ridiculous price of £15,159.13.9d. One wonders what the 9d. (3.75p) was for!

Construction proceeded apace. Materials were delivered in September 1878 and by early December 1879 the railway, 7 miles, 52 chains was ready for inspection by General Hutchinson for the Board of Trade. The Midland themselves supplied the signalling for the line, at a cost recorded as £3,200. The company also supplied the materials for the permanent way, although these were laid down by the contractor.

The Manchester South District Railway opened for local traffic on Thursday, January 1st. 1880. Timetables for this period show

Manchester Central, December 31st.1966: Alongside platform 4, just inside the train shed, history is in the making. The winter daylight glistens off the rain-soaked platform as the train crew chat above the gentle hiss of escaping steam from their engine. This is not just the end of another year, this is the end of a whole era as Class 5 No.**44830** awaits departure with the 12.35 p.m. stopping train to Cheadle Heath. The stock is believed to have consisted of a set of green ex-Southern Railway corridor coaches. After arrival in Cheadle Heath, the Class 5 worked the train empty stock back to Cornbrook Carriage sidings. That day, another chapter in the South District line's history was written, for this is the last regular steam working over this historic stretch of railway.   *W.A.Brown*

fourteen Up locals from Manchester Central and the same number Down from Stockport Tiviot Dale into "Town." Motive power for the local services was in the hands of Mr.S.W.Johnson's 0-4-4 and 0-6-0 tanks. Now at the end of their tether at London Road, The Midland began to run expresses into Manchester Central via Stockport on Monday, August 2nd, 1880. Johnson's elegant slim boilered 4-4-0s were in use on the expresses, double-headed as required. Various members of the numerous Midland 2-4-0 tender classes have been photographed on the line towards the end of the nineteenth century; these have included the elegant "1400" Class and members of the rebuilt Kirtley "800" series built originally for the Settle and Carlisle line. Johnson's superb "Singles" were also used and later on the whole gamut of Midland 4-4-0 power has been recorded at work including the Deeley rebuilds of the Johnson 4-4-0s, the 3Ps-originally built in 1900-and, of course, the celebrated Midland "Compounds."

Interesting aspects of competition began to fringe onto the Midland's services into Manchester in later years. Whatever the vagaries of Victorian industrialism, monopoly power in transport was not one of them. The Great Northern, one of the partners in the CLC, set their sights firmly on Manchester-bound traffic in the 1890s. As we have seen, they had a long-standing working arrangement with the M.S.& L in sharing through services from London Road to King's Cross. With the arrival of the last decade of the nineteenth century the M.S.& L. were to transpose themselves from a cross-country provincial line into the last of the railway "Greats"-the Great Central.

Sir Edward Watkin, one of the truly great Victorian visionaries, had seen the possibility of a trunk line to the Capital and from there to the Continent. Truly, there is nothing new under the sun, and Watkin's idea of a tunnel under the English Channel and through trains from Manchester to Paris, seen as crackpot schemes even until comparatively recently, have a splendid touch of irony in them nowadays.

In October 1891 the M.S.& L. opened their Manchester Central Station Railway from a junction with the South District at Chorlton-cum-Hardy to Fallowfield and then on to Fairfield on the Manchester-Sheffield line the following year. Parallel with the opening of the section to Fallowfield, ownership of the railway north of the junction at Chorlton was transferred (as had been agreed in 1876) from the Midland to the CLC. [M.S.& L. R. (Additional Powers) Act 1886 and Midland Railway (Additional Powers) Act 1887].

For the Midland it was business as before. But now the Great Northern, a previously unwilling partner in the Manchester South District scheme, came back into the Manchester scene. Just across from Manchester Central lay a district known as Alport Town. In today's parlance this area was one vast, unwholesome slum. History does not recall what happened to the inhabitants of Back Lad Lane, of Whitworth Court or of the workers at the Alport Lead Mill. Whatever their eventual lot, it can have been little worse than that they must have endured. Fronting onto Deansgate, and with the Manchester and Salford Junction Canal running through it, it was to this part of the city that the King's Cross company arrived in 1897. The vast Deansgate Goods warehouse covered approximately 9 acres. The site, built on two levels with a massive four-square blue brick building for the interchange of freight, cost the G.N. about £1M, a colossal sum of money in those days. Offices for the collection of parcels had been opened around the town, and the day the Great Central opened its London Extension line for passenger traffic, March 15th. 1899, the first of the Great Northern's own passenger expresses steamed out of Central station for King's Cross. These trains used the South District line to Stockport, then travelled via Brinnington and Bredbury junctions to Woodley; on

then via Apethorne Junction to Godley Junction to traverse the Great Central main line to Sheffield from whence south via Retford to King's Cross.

Later on, in August 1906, the company introduced specially-built 4-coach trains for its independent Manchester service, so highly-valued was the traffic from this northern metropolis at that time. Indeed, speaking in an article in the Railway Magazine in 1906, a writer confidently extolled the possibilty of the Great Northern building its own independent line into Manchester-boldness indeed!

Coming north, Midland trains heading for Manchester topped the summit of the line at Peak Forest, due east of Buxton and standing at 985 feet above sea-level. Almost since leaving Derby, passengers could admire beauty and splendour a-plenty from their carriage window on what was arguably one of the most scenic railway lines in the United Kingdom. From Derbyshire and into Cheshire, the Midland ran through Marple and Romiley into the Market town of Stockport before traversing the flatland flanking the River Mersey, through a still rural south Manchester and into that great northern city-the nineteenth century Mecca of cotton and engineering.

At Marple something of a bottleneck had occured; the station had been enlarged in 1875 to cope with demands for increased local and freight traffic. In the same year a short section of line had been built from Romiley to a junction at Bredbury to join the CLC lines down from Godley Junction and Hyde. This short piece of railway had, of course, given the Midland the necessary access to Manchester Central via the South District line but had opened up a direct route to Liverpool via the CLC route through Northenden, Skelton and Glazebrook East junctions. Though expedient, the Marple, Romiley, Bredbury and Stockport route was hardly conducive to high-speed running and by the turn of the century yet another route into Manchester was being sought, this time the Midland's fourth attempt to reach Cottonopolis unhindered.

The result was the New Mills and Heaton Mersey Railway facilitated by a Midland Railway Act dated August 6th. 1897. Opened for goods traffic on May 4th. 1902 and for passenger traffic on July 1st. that year, the ten mile line was an expensive proposition. Leaving the G.C. & Midland Jt. line at New Mills South Junction, a 3,866 yard tunnel was needed at Disley. Stations were provided at Hazel Grove and at Cheadle Heath, a suburb of Stockport. Facilities at Cheadle Heath bordered on the lavish: five platform faces, a loco turntable and water column, carriage sidings and a large goods depot. Parallel with the opening of the line, another short section-from Cheadle Heath to the CLC main line-gave access to the same stretch of railway facilitated by the Bredbury curve of 1875. Truly, the Midland did nothing by halves.

Another important piece of Midland expansionist policy in the 1880s was the opening, on July 1st.1889, of a short length of railway (¾ mile) from Ancoats Junction (on the section from Ashburys West-on the M.S & L main line-to the Ancoats goods warehouse) to Midland Junction on the L&Y's line from Miles Platting to Ardwick. Via this useful link through running became possible from the burgeoning Midland system over to Manchester's Victoria station where the L&Y were entrenched in rivalry with the Midland's old adversary, the London & North-Western.

Like London Road, Victoria had undergone a massive increase in traffic which had necessitated the enlargement of the original 1844 station by degrees right up to 1904. The Midland began to run trains from Scotland into Victoria from Hellifield in 1888. With the Ancoats curve open they could now operate services from Marple to Blackburn via Manchester Victoria bringing with them through carriages from St.Pancras. By stealth, did the Midland conquer.

With its high-speed and easily-graded line through Disley Tunel open for traffic, a fine terminus almost in the heart of the city of Manchester and a superb hotel to boot, there was just one small length of connecting railway left to complete the South District jigsaw. This was the short, sharply-curved connecting line from Trafford Park Junction on the C.L.C. Liverpool line round to a junction with the South District at the oddly-named Throstle Nest South Junction. This connection gave the Midland company (and, of course, now the Great Central) direct access to the extensive freight sidings at Trafford Park. This 44-chain railway, opened on October 1st. 1906, involved the partial opening-out of both Throstle Nest and Trafford Park tunnels and cost £24,737.15.5d.

In common with almost all mainline stations in those heady years Manchester Central station was enlarged to cope with the demands of increased traffic. On the station's south-east flank, fronting onto Lower Mosley Street, two further platforms-numbered 8 and 9-were built in 1906. These had timber surfaces and were covered with awnings of a short, straight pattern painted in a two-tone finish characteristic of contemporary C.L.C. practice. In common with its southern counterpart, St.Pancras, Central Station was to have had its own hotel incorporated into the station frontage along with offices, booking hall and waiting rooms. This never materialised of course, although the compromise was a magnificent one-the splendidly opulent Midland Hotel, its polished marble facings hiding an interior of unashamed Edwardian poshness.

The frontage of Central station has wrought something of a legend. Whilst a decision pending construction of the hotel complex was made, wooden booking offices of a "temporary" nature were built. These survived up to the station's closure! The luxury Midland Hotel was built on land bordering onto the far side of Windmill Street by the Midland's architect Charles Trubshaw assisted by William Towle. Taking four years to complete, the hotel was built on land purchased in 1896-a considerable time had elapsed after the station's opening-for £365,000. The building, costing £1.25M and opened on September 5th. 1903, was connected by a covered way from the station itself. Thus was completed a remarkable development of railway empire building. In a little over twenty years in an

area where living conditions would almost have defied belief by today's standards, there had grown up a large terminus, with its own separate goods warehouses and office building, a huge goods and office complex, and a hotel, the like of which had never been seen in Manchester before. The Midland knew how to spoil its passengers.

Mention of luxury appendages to rail travel brings to mind the Midland company's involvement with one George Mortimer Pullman, an American who had very radical ideas about how people could be transported in style on the railway. Sir James Allport, then Midland Chairman, had visited the U.S.A. in 1872 and was so impressed with Pullman's carriages that he imported the vehicles (the Americans of course called them "cars")into England, and in early 1874 the Midland ran Pullman cars for the first time.

Though they are long-forgotten now, it is interesting to look back at timetables for the heady years of the South District line in 1885. A journey from Manchester Central to St.Pancras took a leisurely 4 hours, 25 minutes at that time; a Pullman Parlour Car ("Drawing Room Car" had been the earlier title) was attached in the centre of the train. Typically, this would be hauled by one of Mr.Johnson's slim-boilered 4-4-0 locomotives and would consist of some six vehicles. Our pictures will show one such example at speed near Didsbury. The best journey time appears to have been made by the "Special London Express" which left Central at midday and arrived in the Capital at 4.15. Two other Up through trains were also shown as containing Pullmans at that time, but perhaps the piece de resistance was the 5.15 p.m. from Manchester Central which carried a Pullman Dining Saloon Car and arrived in St.Pancras at 9.40.

Connections to and from Liverpool were an essential part of Midland services to the North-West at this time. Trains were divided and made up at Chinley. The station at this Derbyshire village was substantially enlarged and had assumed considerable importance upon the opening of the cut-off line via Disley Tunnel in 1902. From Chinley the Liverpool portions could be run via Cheadle Heath North Junction or via Stockport Tiviot Dale down to and over the CLC Godley to Glazebrook line and thence forward

Central Station, July 25th.1949: Making a brisk start out of the station and round the famous curved approach lines is former LNER D9 4-4-0 No.**62333** with a Liverpool express. The first coach is a Cheshire Lines non-corridor vehicle; the company had its own coaches and wagons, but never locomotives. Passengers wanting to travel from Manchester to Liverpool had a bewildering choice of routes, even in the post-War era. The CLC line, though, had a splendid reputation for punctuality; the company advertised it as "the punctual service" and many Mancunians, my father included, would use no other route. The pre-War standard timing was 45 minutes inclusive of stops at Warrington and Farnworth (now Widnes); this had fallen back to 53 minutes at the time this picture was taken.

P.Ward

into Liverpool Central. In 1885, again, we see portions of through trains with Pullman Parlour Car attached leaving Liverpool at 11.00 a.m., joining at Tiviot Dale at 11.35 with St.Pancras reached at 4.15. A further venture into luxury travel was the Pullman Sleeping Car. These, too, were a feature of Midland trains in that first decade. Services left the two cities, Liverpool and Manchester, at 11.20 and 11.50 respectively. Both contained Sleepers and joined at Stockport; arrival in St.Pancras was at 5.15 a.m.

By 1904, with the "cut-off" line via Disley in operation, Midland London-Manchester express timings were almost rivalling those of the London & North-Western. The latter, albeit with heavier trains, were managing Euston-London Road times of 3½ hours at best. Over on the Midland route 3 hours 40, to 3 hours 50 minutes was established, a considerable improvement on the 4 hours, 15 minutes and 4 hours, 25 minutes of 1885. Though the Midland engines were hauling lighter trains, the route possessed severe gradients almost throughout-the summit at Peak Forest, at 985 feet above sea-level being the piece de resistance. Apart from the initial severity of the 1-in-75 climb out of Euston up Camden Bank, the London & North-Western had an easy job of it.

Before the First War the fastest Midland down trains avoided Derby via the Chaddesden curve and stopped only at Leicester. Going up, non-stop runs were made over the 175.1 miles from Chinley to St.Pancras and from even as far north as Cheadle Heath-186.9 miles from London. What is interesting is that both runs were made via the Dore and Chinley line and Chesterfield, anticipating modern practice whereby certain cross-country Liverpool to East Anglia services use a portion of the same route. Oh that we could travel through to St.Pancras via Inter-City from Manchester today!

As a footnote it is worth recalling that in the halcyon summer of 1914 the Midland ran non-stop expresses from St.Pancras to Liverpool upon the opening of the Adelphi Hotel. From Chinley the expresses, 6.10 p.m. ex St.Pancras, ran via Cheadle Heath and the Liverpool Curve down to the CLC line at Cheadle Junction, then to Glazebrook to join the Manchester-Liverpool line. The time taken was 4 hours, 10 minutes for the 217¾ miles. There is something valedictory in that little tale; one last gesture, one final flourish from one of the great pre-1923 railway companies before it, and much of the civilised world, was caught up in the awful conflict known as the First World War. Those four dreadful years formed something of a watershed in European civilisation; forming a wedge between the old order of Victorian and Edwardian England and that which was to follow: the Grouping of 1923, and the onset of social and economic changes which were to ultimately result in the loss, not only of their identity, but also of much of the railways' monopoly power in inland transport.

In the post-1923 years the rivalry between the two routes-London & North-Western and Midland-ceased, of course, to exist; though it was Derby who dominated in the field of motive power development for some years. In this period the Midland route came to be looked on in a different context: that of relieving the Western Division main line of some of its traffic. Over on the erstwhile Midland, Derby was now considered too important to miss-with London-Manchester trains stopping both there and at Leicester. Chinley, too, was included in the case of trains carrying a through portion for Liverpool.

The latter days of the Midland had seen the main Manchester expresses leave St.Pancras at twenty-five minutes past the hour-giving them the unofficial title of "Twenty-Fives." Come October 1937 express departures were altered to half-past the hour, and in 1938 a spate of train naming broke out. Two names were used for expresses between St.Pancras and Manchester. Leaving London, the 10.30 morning train took the title "Peak Express" and covered

the journey, including stops at Derby and Leicester, in 3 hours, 35 minutes and restoring at last the best times of Midland days. "The Palatine" was the name bestowed on the second named express. This left St.Pancras at 4.30 p.m. and included a stop at Bedford as well as stops at Matlock, Chinley and Cheadle Heath. Arrival in Manchester Central was at 8.12 p.m. making an overall running time of 3 hours, 47 minutes.

In the reverse direction "The Palatine" left Manchester Central at 10.00 a.m. and called at Cheadle Heath, Derby and Leicester. St.Pancras was reached at 1.48-a timing of 3 hours, 48 minutes. "The Peak Express" departed from Manchester at 4.25 p.m. and was booked non-stop to Derby. On this service Loughborough, Leicester and Luton were called at with the train due into St.Pancras at 8.12 p.m.-a scheduled time of 3 hours, 47 minutes, just one minute's difference from that of "The Palatine." Looking back at those pre-War schedules it seems strange that today none of those important former calling places-Bedford, Derby, Leicester, Loughborough and Luton-are thought worthy of any direct Inter-City service to Manchester.

The outbreak of the Second War, as everywhere else, brought ruin upon the timings of the Manchester-London services over the Midland line. Journey times lengthened to between 5¼ and 5¾ hours with an improvement to 4 hours, 18 minutes and 4 hours, 38 minutes appearing in 1946. By Summer 1950 there had scarcely been any improvement, with Up schedules at best 4 hours, 28 minutes (1.45 pm ex Central) and Down schedules 4 hours, 32 minutes (2.15 pm ex St.Pancras.) Over on the former LNWR route out of London Road to Euston the prospects for speedier travel were somewhat better: Up trains made the journey almost parallel with the best pre-First War times-3 hours, 38 minutes (the 9.45 a.m. "Mancunian") and the evening (5.50) "Comet" just behind at 3 hours, 46 minutes. Down trains, too, out of Euston also had the edge on their old rivals with the morning "Comet" (9.45) covering the 188 3/4 miles (via Stoke-on-Trent and Macclesfield) in just 3 1/2 hours. In fairness it should be pointed out that the times of the named trains on the LNWR route were not typical; other journeys took around 4 to 4½ hours, much the same as those on the Midland line. To put these workings into further perspective other things have to be considered: the LNWR route was easily graded (apart from the initial 1 in 75 out of Euston up Camden Bank) whereas the Midland line, as has already been stated, was severely graded throughout-the piece de resistance being the long pull up to Peak Forest at 985 feet above sea level. Conversely, though, Manchester trains on the LNWR line were much more heavily loaded-up to 15 coaches being a common occurence; those on the Midland line more usually around 8 or 9. Again, though, Midland trains never had the benefit of anything greater than Class 5 or 6 motive power up until the arrival of "Britannia" Pacifics in 1958 and, later, Type "4" Diesels. Trains on the Euston line, though sharing the mixture of "Black 5's", "Jubilees", and "Scots" that their Midland rivals used, could often call on Pacifics in the shape of the mighty "Duchesses" and the occasional foray by the solitary Standard Class 8 "Duke of Gloucester."

In order to give readers a fuller picture of the motive power situation on the Manchester St.Pancras expresses in 1950, here is an extract from the signalbox register at Didsbury for part of February and March that year. Thanks to the Midland practice of recording engine numbers carried on by signalman T.B.Archer we have a unique record of locomotive running on these services. The period begins on Thursday, February 23rd. and five trains (all morning ex Manchester Central) are recorded. They are: 7.10 to St.Pancras, 7.24 to Derby, 8.55 to St.Pancras, 10.50 to Chinley and the 11.35 to Nottingham.

DATE	TRAIN	ENGINE NUMBERS
23/2	7.10 to St.Pancras	45649
24/2	"	45628
25/2	"	45655
6/3	"	45652
7/3	"	45553
8/3	"	45655
9/3	"	45641
10/3	"	45629
11/3	"	45618
13/3	"	45632
14/3	"	45629

DATE	TRAIN	ENGINE NUMBER/S
23/2	7.24 to Derby	41055
24/2	"	40900
25/2	"	41055
6/3	"	40910
7/3	"	41181
8/3	"	40910
9/3	"	41181
10/3	"	40910
11/3	"	41181
13/3	"	41076
14/3	"	40910

DATE	TRAIN	ENGINE NUMBER/S
23/2	8.55 to St.Pancras	44851
24/2	"	45627
25/2	"	45673
6/3	"	45618
7/3	"	45618
8/3	"	45652
9/3	"	44818/45629
10/3	"	44726/45655
11/3	"	45655
13/3	"	45618
14/3	"	45696/45553
23/2	10.50 to Chinley	45264
24/2	"	45590
25/2	"	44985

From 6/3 through to 13/3, 44964 worked this train every day.

DATE	TRAIN	ENGINE NUMBER/S
23/2	11.35 to Nottingham	40900
24/2	"	41055
25/2	"	45629
6/3	"	41181
7/3	"	40910
8/3	"	41184
9/3	"	40910
10/3	"	41181
11/3	"	44661

Readers can use their well-thumbed ABCs to turn up the names of the "Jubilees" that plied this route. Worthy of mention is the double-heading of the 8.55 express and the use of "Compounds" on the slower trains, a feature on this line for many years. Until the arrival of the "Scots" from about 1957/58, double-headed expresses were a regular sight along here. I well remember seeing an express from St.Pancras tearing through Didsbury in the early afternoon one Saturday in 1957. The train engine was a "Black 5" with a "2P" as the pilot engine; such was the impression of speed, I thought the whole ensemble looked ready to take off!

Named expresses returned to the Manchester-St.Pancras services in 1957 when the name "Palatine" re-appeared in the timetable. The Down train left St.Pancras at 7.55 a.m. and arrived in Manchester at 11.45. Its Up counterpart was an afternoon departure leaving Manchester Central at 2.25 p.m. and arriving in London at 6.10 p.m. Train watchers on the South District line saw a radical change in motive power when, in the Spring of 1958, six "Britannia" Pacifics arrived at Trafford Park and Kentish Town depots to head many of the London expresses. Later that year Type "4" Diesels came on the scene and the transformation was complete. In 1959 the London Midland region were pushing ahead with electrification of the Manchester-Crewe-Euston line. Sadly, this was to result in the ultimate demise of the South District railway, but before that took place one further upheaval, perhaps one might say revolution, in timetabling occured.

In the late summer of 1962 it was announced that the next winter Midland line timetable would embody the most drastic reconstruction of services ever to take place. The bulk of the Manchester-London trains were to be diverted over the Midland route to St.Pancras. This would compensate for the withdrawal of many of the services from Piccadilly to Euston necessitated by the reconstruction of the London terminal pending electrification.

Train departures from both Central and St.Pancras were in most cases arranged at 25 minutes past each hour. Some slight variations occured, namely the 8.05 from London (the existing 7.55 "Palatine") and the 5.00 and 6.55 p.m. out of St.Pancras as well as the "Midland Pullman"-the 6-coach Diesel-Electric flagship of the route introduced in July 1960-re-scheduled to begin its Down journey at 6.10 p.m. A new service was the 9.25 from St.Pancras, essentially a substitute for the "Comet", which called only at Leicester and Cheadle Heath and bypassed Derby via the Chaddesden avoiding line. This train completed the journey in 3 hours, 35 minutes.

From Manchester Central there was initiated an unbroken hourly sequence of departures for the Capital. Beginning at 7.25 a.m. the service ranged through to 6.25 p.m. and included departures also at 11.25 a.m. and 6.25 p.m. as well as the 7.45 a.m. "Midland Pullman " which covered the distance in a 3 hours, 10 minute slot.

The fastest trains were limited to 9 coaches (320 tons), slower ones to 11 vehicles north of Derby with increased loads of up to 14 coaches (470 tons) between Derby and St.Pancras. Such improved timings and heavier loadings were only made possible by the use throughout of the, then, relatively new "Peak" (aptly enough) 2,500 h.p. Diesels.

An interesting sidelight on the altered service was the transfer of the sleeping car services from the LNW route, not to the Midland line, but to the Great Central main line, Marylebone to Manchester London Road throughout. Even then, rumours of closure of the Great Central route were going around and total eclipse was not far away.

The long-awaited electrification of the London-Manchester route via Crewe and the Potteries came onstream in April 1966. Its work as a diversionary route completed, the Midland line settled down to second division status for a few years more. On the South District line itself, the decline of local services had begun a long time back, perhaps, some might say, long before even the Second War if ticket receipts were taken as the yardstick. July 3rd.1961 saw the simultaneous closure of both Heaton Mersey and Withington and West Didsbury stations. Didsbury and Chorlton-cum-Hardy saw a few more years glory before they, too, succumbed on January 1st. 1967. Stockport Tiviot Dale, with its beautiful Jacobean facade, was also doomed and this fine building closed its doors as well on this New Year day.

Looming on the horizon now was the closure of Manchester Central and the diversion away to either Piccadilly or Oxford Road of all its services. This spectre first appears to have raised its ugly head in a memorandum dated September 29th. 1966 submitted to the London Midland Railway (sic) Board. The memo crystalized the workings in and out of Central and stated that some of the Central services had been scheduled for withdrawal. It then recalled that formal proposals had been made to the T.U.C.C. on June 23rd. recommending that the "remaining" services be diverted to either Piccadilly or Oxford Road.

The next stage in the proceedings came in a report made to the General Manager of the London Midland Region dated 28th. November 1966. This outlined in further detail the broad proposals of the previous report and stated that: "there are no major obstacles to the closure of Manchester Central station but there are various recommendations *for confirmation and in certain cases for decision as between alternatives.*

The main thrust of the report can be detailed as follows:

a) Re-timing of Manchester-London St.Pancras passenger trains via the Midlands. "It may be considered undesirable to re-time some of these trains south of Chinley by virtue of the effect on other services but the disadvantage of re-timing local train services at peak times at the Manchester end must be taken into account in this consideration."
b) The transfer of Manchester-Liverpool trains, along with the Irlam-Manchester local trains, to Oxford Road. The inclusion of stops at Knott Mill (for Deansgate) for these services was put forward as a possibility due to "commercial demand."
c) Improvement of access to and from platforms 13/14 at Piccadilly station along with the elimination of the Wyman's bookstall at this site.
d) Elimination of parcels traffic at Oxford Road station.
e) The provision of additional access at Oxford Road to platforms 1/2 via the subway. It was also proposed to reduce the car parking facilities at this station and to provide only what were described as "short wait" facilities. (The number of trains using Oxford Road would rise from 295 to 350 each day.)
f) The removal of Cornbrook carriage sidings and the re-modelling of the associated junctions. Stock displaced from Cornbrook would be housed at Longsight, Adswood and the Hazel Grove loop.
g) Additional carriage/DMU servicing, fuelling and cleaning facilities would be provided at Longsight. A review of arrangements for cleaning, fuelling and servicing of stock at Cornbrook, Ardwick, Longsight, Reddish and Stockport depots was to be undertaken.
h) The MSJ&A line would be re-signalled between Warwick Road, Cornbrook East and Piccadilly. Signalboxes at Oxford Road, Castlefield Junction, Cornbrook East Junction, Cornbrook West Junction, Throstle Nest East Junction and Old Trafford Junction would be closed. A relay room would be provided at Cornbrook and a power signalling installation would be provided at Throstle Nest East. Subsequently, Throstle Nest South Junction, where the curve from the South District round to the Liverpool line ran off, was closed as well.

As a footnote to the last proposal (h) it was proposed at that time to convert the MSJ&A line to 25 kv ac from the existing 1931 standard of 1500 v dc. The MSJ&A overhead line equipment was then life-expired and its conversion to modern standards, with subsequent integration into the Manchester-Crewe network, was a perfectly logical proposal. Although this formed no part of the 1966 closure remit, the track and signalling requirements at Oxford Road would have been affected by the 25 kv conversion.

It was also recommended that the bridge structures (the Castlefield viaducts) leading to Manchester Central be retained pending their take-over by Manchester City Council for "road traffic." A sum of £197,000 was quoted in the report for their removal. £25,000 p.a. was quoted for maintenance if the viaducts remained in railway use, £1,000 p.a. to keep them in a safe condition "pending removal." The possibility of the council providing a "bus-way" over the bridges is also mentioned. It was, indeed, very fortunate that these magnificent structures were not removed as, without them, the current "Metrolink" (LRT) route could never (literally) have got off the ground, such would have been the cost of providing a replacement structure.

A target date of June 1968 was set for the closure programme to be realised. Attainment of this, however, was dependent on the requisite engineering work being completed in the ensuing eighteen months. The necessary work for the Central station closure was estimated at £539,000. Of this total, £225,000 was set aside for signalling and telecommunications, £197,00 for the removal of 24 underbridges between Central Station and Cornbrook, £66,000 for alterations to stabling, cleaning and re-fuelling facilities for DMUs and rolling stock, £48,000 for alterations to stations and structures. Work to permanent way worked out at just £3,000-a mere bagatelle. A consequent decrease in working expenses of £424,000 was predicted; of this sum, £85,000 would be saved on repairs, £34,000 on renewals, £48,000 on operating expenses and £257,000 on staff. The latter were described in the report (perhaps somewhat cynically) as "219 units." A return on the net outlay was shown as yielding 79%. The B.R. accountants had a field day when, at the foot of the report, they showed land released for development to have a realisable value of £2M for the Central site and £750,000 for the site at Cornbrook. £2.75M was an awful lot of money in 1966.

And, sadly, the plans were set in motion. Whatever one may think of the Central closure, reading through the various pages of minutes relating to it one cannot fail but be impressed by the total thoroughness of the whole thing and the military-style detail, with progress reports and meetings to ensure all went smoothly. Doubts had been expressed initially that consent by the Ministry of Transport to the closure was by no means certain. As late as February, 1969 a meeting was held at Cornbrook Carriage Sidings and it is written that: "*The board is under obligation to re-open Manchester (Central) passenger station if the alternative passenger services are not satisfactory. Therefore, until M.O.T. permission is received to remove the formation, all land will remain operational.*"

Expresses to Nottingham and London St.Pancras continued to run from Central until January 1st. 1968 when they were re-routed to Manchester Piccadilly. All the Up services ran on the later Great Central and Midland Joint line via Reddish. All bar one Down train stayed on former Midland metals; this was 3H03, the 20.20 (SX) St.Pancras to Stockport (Postal) which was re-routed via Crewe to Stockport Edgeley.

Thus had the wheel come full circle and Midland line trains arrived back at platform faces adjacent to where they had stood at some 112 years previously! With a meagre two trains per week each up and down the South District line, total eclipse here now loomed large. The trains in question were Sundays only services between Liverpool Lime Street and Sheffield Midland via Manchester Central.

The official closure date for Manchester Central was set for May 5th. 1969. This was a Monday, traffic into and out of the terminus had actually ceased on Saturday, May 3rd. Some doubt exists as to the exact date of the last passenger traffic over the South District line; one source gives Sunday, May 4th., another Sunday, April 27th.

Odd freight trains continued to operate from the Cheadle Heath direction to and from Trafford Park but, as the summer of 1969 progressed, this fine stretch of railway was doomed. The connections at Chorlton Junction were severed on August 17th. and by October all the track had gone right through up to Didsbury and Heaton Mersey. (The original 1880 section from Heaton Mersey Station along to Heaton Mersey East had closed completely on January 2nd. 1967).

Chorlton-cum-Hardy (could there ever have been a more English-spounding name?) was razed to the ground to become a Safeway supermarket development. Withington and West Didsbury station and its fine cobbled forecourt was sold to a property developer, flats known as "Lapwing Court" now cover the ground where the fine Victorian buildings with their quaint, almost ecclesiastical air once stood. Didsbury was luckier, the buildings there did duty as a hardware shop until 1980 when they, too, were demolished. Unluckiest of all was Heaton Mersey where the cutting was entombed in a landfill operation, to be perhaps uncovered as that fine writer, Raymond Keeley, has said "in some archaeological dig in a thousand years." The high-level bridge which took the the 1902 cut-off line high over the Mersey was removed soon after. Rationalisation had won the day.

The Central station site languished, unloved and unwanted, for over an entire decade as a car-park-the ultimate irony that has befallen so many railway buildings. Owned for a while by the NCP empire, the place rapidly became rundown and it seemed as though the long-awaited exhibition hall complex was never to be. Then, in the early 1980s, the magic word "Jarvis" appeared on a hoarding over that great 90 foot high roof span, and salvation was at hand.

Like a Phoenix arisen from the ashes, the G-Mex (Greater Manchester Exhibition Centre) centre opened in the Spring of 1986 to much acclaim. Still it is possible to gaze up at that magnificent roof, still we can imagine the sights and sounds of steam and Diesel. Still, the ghosts of *"Ypres"*, *"Mons"*, *"Hong Kong"* and even *"Iron Duke"* have not been exorcised by the march of time. As this introduction is penned, an overhead catenary has appeared alongside the centre and once more the environs resound to the rumble of steel wheels on rail. Now they are called "Light Rail Vehicles", but at least one of those splendid viaducts is, again, fulfilling its original purpose.

One could conclude that, had the Midland not been ousted from London Road in the 1870s, then they would never have needed to use the alignment of the South District Railway, we would not have had Manchester Central-or the Midland Hotel and the railway map of Manchester would have been totally different. But history, of course, is not like that. Decisions are taken in the light of events of the time, they reflect the judgements of men, they mirror their hopes and aspirations. The Midland Railway was, not for nothing, ambitious, single-minded and determined. As Hamilton Ellis reminded us, "The Midland was a magnificent railway."

E.M.Johnson,
Burnage, Manchester, July 1992.

Midland Hotel. c.1903. The familiar Wyverne and the famous name stand out clearly here: a bold thrusting commercial venture by a company that knew what it was doing - and did it well. The hotel was brand-new when this picture, looking across from St.Peter's Square, was taken. Built on a scale that even today is breathtaking, the hotel exudes luxury and opulence. Though no longer in railway hands, one benefit of the recent sell-off to the American-owned Holiday Inn chain has been the restoration of the original foyer and entrance, clearly visible here, to its early Edwardian splendour.   *Author's collection*

Manchester Central, Wednesday, January 18th.1956: One of a series of pictures taken showing the extension to the station which opened in April 1906. This was situated on the station's south-easterly side and fronted onto Lower Mosley Street.

a) A view from Lower Mosley Street showing the refreshment rooms, quite a pleasant match with the architecture of the rest of the station. Two valuable extra platforms were provided by this later building as well as a carriage road and extra office space. Here, too, was a separate side entrance to the station, just visible by the MCTC bus stage. The second storey of the building provided refreshment services for passengers in the form of a cafeteria and bar. That Edwardian masterpiece, the Midland Hotel dominates the view over Windmill Street in the background. The Humber saloon car-HUN 1 must have belonged to a railway enthusiast; the keen-eyed may be able to pick out the "Number 1" oval wagon plate carrying the words "Festiniog Railway" and mounted to the left of the radiator grille. *British Transport Commission*

b) Looking down Lower Mosley Street towards Whitworth Street and Chester Road we see the bridge provided to carry the two extra platform roads over Bridgewater Street. After closure the station extension, along with the CLC goods warehouses and this bridge were razed to the ground leaving the original 1880 building to stand alone. Then, with the advent of the "Metrolink" LRT scheme, it was decided that another bridge would be needed to carry the new system, and Bridgewater Street was bridged once more. Strange, indeed, the way history repeats itself! Again, railway historians can look back at the excursion programme of the time. On offer just over 36 years ago on Sunday, 29th. January were trips to Sheffield (5/6d), Peterborough (16/-), Wolverhampton (9/-), Leamington Spa (12/6d) and Lancaster (7/3d). *British Transport Commission*

c) A third look at the extension building showing all ten arched windows with corresponding openings on the upper storey. Here we are standing on the far left of the station forecourt looking down the carriage road which backed onto the rear of platform 9 giving direct access for loading. *British Transport Commission*

Manchester Central, May 1969: Two minutes past six sees the station frontage on the weekend of closure, the magnificent arched roof now almost at the end of its life–at least as far as railway purposes allow. To the left are the wooden ticket offices, the "temporary" structures that lasted to the end of the station's existence. The photographer is stood in the middle of Mount Street, then home of the Divisional Civil Engineer. A British Railways hoarding to the right of the gate pillars exorts potential trippers to "travel like a king" to London for a day's outing. Such delights as Crufts Dog Show, the Boat Race and the Ideal Home Exhibition are flaunted to tempt the traveller. Vintage transport touches are provided by the sight of A Ford Corsair, a Jaguar Mark X, a Ford Anglia and a Mark I Ford Escort. Passengers (the abominable "customers" had yet to arrive) could park on the forecourt for a mere 2/6d, "Others" were charged 5/- (25p). *M.S.Welch*

Manchester Central 12th May 1959: Though this picture was used before in my " Manchester Railway Termini" book I thought it would be nice to include it again on an enlarged scale. Taken from a high vantage point near the clock that stood at the back of the arched roof, no other interior view captures such a wealth of interior detail. The 210 foot roof span, 90 feet above rail level was the design of one H.L.Moorson who had been appointed Resident Engineer for Station Works, Manchester in 1872. Robert Neill, along with Andrew Handyside & Co. of Derby, were responsible for the substructure and roof respectively. A feature of the track layout from the outset was the provision of the loco release roads-accessed from each of the

platform roads via "Y" switches. These were hand-operated and the centre roads themselves were not track-circuited. At platform six, on the left-hand side of the view, a 2-6-4 tank draws away after delivering a train of empty corridor carriages-almost certain to be an express for St.Pancras. Through the arches in the train shed wall alongside the express the traveller alighted straight onto platform 8. This caused some confusion, many people thinking platform 7 had disappeared! Not so, the latter was a bay between 6 and 8; the rear of a carriage standing in the "lost" platform can just be glimpsed alongside the fifth vehicle of the express. *British Rail*

Midland Hotel. c.1905. Reproduced from a postcard that was dispatched to a Mrs Stevenson of Gorton Road, Reddish on June 26th 1906, this is the rear of the hotel viewed from the Central Station forecourt. The horse and cart inevitably dominates as the prime mover and the covered way that connected the station with the rear of the hotel has yet to be extended.   *Author's collection*

Manchester Central n.d: A pre-War scene showing something of the opposite side of the approach with a fine array of vintage motor vehicles. The buildings to the left of the view were parcels offices, those to the right formed part of a small complex which fronted onto Watson Street and were Goods warehouses belonging to the Cheshire Lines Committee. They survived intact after the station closed and did duty as inevitable car parking space before being demolished in May 1978.

Collection of R.G.Chapman

Manchester Central n.d: It was once said of the Midland Railway that: "it actually seemed to like passengers-a rare virtue in any transport undertaking." This waggish statement is given credence here in this, another pre-War view of the station frontage. Witness the fine wrought iron and glass canopy stretching from the front of the station, over the forecourt and across Windmill Street to connect the front of the station directly with the Midland Hotel. The special entrance provided for passengers can be seen to this day, but the canopy, along with the Daily Dispatch has long since passed into history.   *Collection of R.G.Chapman*

Manchester Central n.d: An opposite end view to those of the station frontage showing clearly details of the station goods yard and its associated signalling. No date is available for this picture, but it is likely to have been taken sometime in 1935 when the revised signalling scheme was put into operation-witness the colour light signal waiting to supplant the CLC-pattern semaphores by the second LMS wagon. Visible under the Town Hall clock is the twin arched roof of the goods station; the associated goods warehouse can be seen to the left.
G.H.Platt

Manchester Central, 1920s: A vintage panorama looking down along platform 6 and showing a busy station; both clerestory and elliptical-roofed coaching stock is in evidence. "Read the Manchester Guardian" extols the poster hoarding above Messrs.W.H.Smith's bookstall. Above the stall the "Thrilling Amateur T.T.Races" (resumed in 1920 after the First War) are proclaimed as an attraction on the Isle of Man. Notice the passage through the archway on the left-hand side pointing passenger to platforms 8 and 9. The "missing" platform was number 7- the bay at the top of platform 6. *Author's collection*

Manchester Central. c.1904. Unfortunately, it is not possible to positively identify this Johnson Midland Class 3 4-4-0 "Belpaire" leaving the station with a southbound express. However, this particular member of the class is thought to be from a group numbered **2606-10** which was changed to **700-704** in 1907. Numerous modifications were carried out to the locomotives over the years, the last engine of a total of eighty being withdrawn in 1953.
Collection J. Braithwaite.

Manchester Central early 1912: Until June 1935 signalling at Manchester Central had been controlled by four separate signalboxes. These were known as "A", "B", "Great Northern Junction", and "Viaduct." Some fine photographs exist showing, mostly, Great Central locomotives standing in front of the largest of these boxes-"B" signalbox which stood on the south-east side of the station, in front of the water tower and at the back of the turntable roads. Of the pictures available I selected this one as it gives the best clear view of at least part of the signalbox-a typically large CLC structure with a gabled roof and very characteristic divided window arrangement, sections of two small upper windows split by a horizontal sash from two large lower ones and divided into six groups separated by a large brick chimney. The locomotive is one of the M.S.& L's Class 2 6'-9" 4-4-0s built originally in 1887 to a design by Thomas Parker for haulage of the joint M.S.& L/G.N. Manchester London Road-King's Cross expresses. No.**565** was built at Gorton in August 1890 and was rebuilt by the Great Central's J.G.Robinson in November 1911 to the form seen here with a raised boiler and Belpaire firebox. Robinson also provided the handsome chimney and extended smokebox. Later in their lives the Class 2s (LNER D7) received extended cab roofs (a process not begun until 1912 which helps to date the picture) and coal plates to their tenders. As LNER No. 5565 this fine specimen was withdrawn in April 1933.   *Author's collection*

Manchester Central c.1899: S.W.Johnson joined the Midland Railway in 1873 from the Great Eastern and set about producing the first of a very elegant series of 4-4-0s from 1876 onwards. No.**2217** was one of the later series-one of 45 engines of the "2203" or "O" Class with 6'-6" coupled wheels built variously between 1893 and 1895. Her crimson lake body colour positively gleaming and with glowing brasswork, No.2217 stands on the turntable outside the station-"B" signalbox is glimpsed again in the background. The quintessence of Victorian engineering, these magnificent engines would have been deployed on expresses to Nottingham, and St.Pancras at the time this picture was taken. The headlamp code related to Up Midland expresses over the South District line-it was some years before an almost unified lamp code was adopted.
Collection of W.G.Rear

Manchester Central c.1899: All the hustle and bustle of the Victorian railway scene is gathered together in this splendid view of a Sacré's Class 14 2-2-2 (possibly No.**109**) making a boisterous start out of the terminus with an express, almost certainly bound for Liverpool. Steam issues from the sanding gear, safety valves lift, and a copious exhaust billows high into the air. Across in the goods yard a shunting engine is busy whilst alongside a Midland 0-4-4 tank engine waits impatiently. Charles Sacre' introduced his Class 14 7'-6" Single-wheeler in 1882, a further 11 engines were turned out from Gorton Works the following year. Originally conceived for hauling the joint MSL/GN expresses between Manchester and Grantham, the entire class migrated to the Cheshire Lines system from 1887 where they worked the bulk of the fast Liverpool trains to and from Manchester Central. Destined for a short life, all the Class 14s had gone by the end of 1907.

Collection of W.G.Rear

Manchester Central March 15th 1899: At around the turn of the century no less than four separate railway companies were competing for the London-Manchester passenger traffic. Though the Great Northern, in partnership with the M.S.& L., had long worked through trains between the two cities, the opening of the Great Central's (late M.S.& L.) line through to Marylebone gave the Great Northern the impetus it needed to operate through trains of its own. Wednesday, March 15th 1899 was the chosen day, the same day the Great Central's London Extension opened for passenger traffic. Seen leaving platform 6 on that historic day is Ivatt G.N.R. Class D2 ("400" Class) No.**1343** making a brisk start with the 2.05 p.m. express to King's Cross. It is known the engine worked to Grantham and returned to Central on a Down train from King's Cross, due in at 10.14 pm. No. 1343 had been built the previous year and was one of a batch of 4-4-0s sent to Trafford Park shed (numbered 11 by the G.N.) especially to work these services. Even by pre-Group standards the engine is well turned-out. A mirror finish has been imparted to the rich green paintwork with chocolate brown underframes and lamps, buffers, coupling chains and lubricators have been polished to perfection. Notice the crowd of onlookers-something tremendous is thought to be afoot here! The initial G.N. through service consisted of five trains daily. Departures began in the morning at 10.10, and continued at 12.10, 2.05, 5.00 and 11.05 p.m. The 2.05 train, along with the other four departures, traversed the South District and CLC lines described in the introduction. The 5.0'clock train differed from the others in that it travelled via Nottingham.

Collection of W.G.Rear

Manchester Central. n.d: Deeley "Flatiron" 0-6-4 tank No. **2002** is about to depart from platform 5 with a South District line Local. This view that shows off the rather handsome curved wooden valancing of the platform canopies. No. 2002 appears to be breaking something of a general rule with these engines which invariably worked "chimney out"-"bunker in" on South District Locals. Enthusiasts in the Manchester area dubbed the Deeley 0-6-4s "Woofle Tanks" on account of the somewhat muffled tones of their exhausts. "Block Tanks" appears to be another sobriquet applied to them. Introduced by Deeley in 1907 these 0-6-4 locos had a mixed press on account of their reported instability at speed. They were a relatively short lived species by Midland standards, all had gone by 1938.   *Author's collection*

Manchester Central c.1899: Standing on the loco release road between platforms 3 and 4 is Johnson 0-4-4 tank No. **1533**. These handsome engines worked South District line local services along with (inter alia) the larger Johnson 0-6-0 tanks until the advent of the Deeley 0-6-4 "Flatirons" in 1907. No. 1533 was a member of the "1532" Class first built at Derby in 1881. Re-numbered 1267 in the 1907 scheme, 1533 lasted through the LMS period and into BR days.

Collection of W.G.Rear

Manchester Central 1880s: One of the earliest pictures taken at Manchester Central would appear to be this one showing Sacré Class 12 2-4-0 6'-3" express engine No. **314.** Seen standing alongside platform 4, this fine example of Victorian locomotive engineering was built at Gorton Works in June 1873. Her duties out of Central in this period would almost certainly have taken in express working to Liverpool. Finished in the M.S.& L. livery of dark green, with chocolate frames and polished brass fittings, these fine specimens must have been a sight to behold-though pity the poor loco crews who must have suffered badly in adverse weather with what was a mere apology for a cab. Projecting from the smokebox are the twin pipes for the Smith simple vacuum brake used by the M.S.& L. at this time until around 1889. No. 314 was withdrawn in May 1916 as 314B.

Author's collection

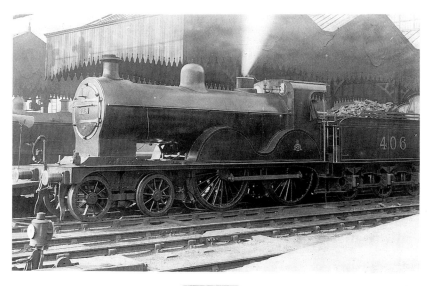

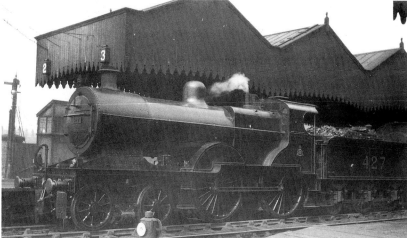

Manchester Central n.d: Under the regime of R.M.Deeley the slender, almost Classical lines of the Johnson 4-4-0s began to disappear. Deeley rebuilt Johnson's "2183" Class with his own higher-pitched "H" class boilers between 1906 and 1908. The result is manifest here in this view of the former No. **2186**, now re-numbered 406, alongside platform 5 awaiting departure with an up express over the South District line. Clerestory stock of the non-corridor variety is visible behind the tender in the original photo. Clearly seen too, is the striped awning over the platforms with the original elegantly-shaped woodwork. Peeping out along-side platform 3 is another "Flatiron"-number unknown- breaking the "chimney out" rule. The "2183" Class were again rebuilt, with Belpaire fireboxes, in the period 1914-1922. In this guise they lasted until modern times, some examples seeing service into the late 1950s. *Author's collection*

Manchester Central n.d: A view in the later Midland Railway era shows the full extent of the rebuilding of the Johnson 4-4-0 "2183" Class with Belpaire fireboxes and flat footplating. Clearly taken alongside platform 3 we see No. **427**, formerly No.2202, awaiting departure with a train of corridor stock. Notice the wooden platforms, still extant, along with the fully curved wooden valancing to the canopies; the small signal box in the goods yard is the "A" box referred to previously.

Author's collection

Manchester Central pre WW1: An interesting contrast to the view of the "Director" is provided by this picture of Great Central Class 3 (LNE F1) 2-4-2 tank engine No. **591**. Notice here that the water tower lacks the bays cut into the base in later years to provide accommodation for bigger locomotives. The Class 3 locos were introduced in 1889 to a design by Thomas Parker specifically for local passenger services in the Manchester area. In later years two of these charming little engines acted as station pilots here at Central. All were eventually fitted with Belpaire fireboxes from 1909 onwards; No. 591 received hers in August 1915. Brass oval numberplates had been fitted from around 1912 and all the engines ultimately acquired J.G.Robinson's hand-some chimney, something of a relief to the austere stovepipe seen here. No. 591 was withdrawn in March, 1934.

Author's collection

Manchester Central c.1913/14: Alongside platform 5 and ready for the "off" is one of J.G.Robinson's flagship express passenger engines-No. **425** *"City of Manchester"* in typically spotless pre- Group condtion. The Great Central Class 1 4-6-0 (LNE B2) had appeared at the end of 1912. The prototype, No. 423 "Sir Sam Fay" was named after the Great Central's Chairman and five other engines to the same design appeared the following year named after cities served by the company. No. 423 would have been heading over the Fallowfield line from Chorlton Junction soon after this picture was taken. Though the class were used initially on the GC's London trains from both Central and London Road, they were soon transferred to cross-country workings via Sheffield to Lincoln, Hull and Harwich. "City of Manchester" was withdrawn in July 1947   *Author's collection*

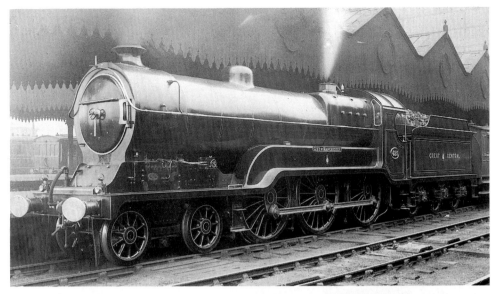

Manchester Central c.1899: Although engines of the LNER constituent companies did not, by and large, venture south of Chorlton Junction-photographs showing the full extent of the canopies and arched roof at the turn of the century are so rare as to make the inclusion of this picture a "must." Another of Sacré's 6B 4-4-0s, this time No.129 of 1880, stands in the centre road between platforms 5 and 6. The engine makes an interesting contrast with No. 440-still with stovepipe chimney, from the Parker regime, and earlier pattern smokebox. The platform canopies are still in their original form: curved edges with a sawtooth pattern and moulded roundels in the centre of each ridge. In later years, around the early 1930s, these elegant edges to the canopies were cut off to leave a straight edge. Notice that the platforms themselves were still made out of wood at this time.   *Collection of W.G.Rear*

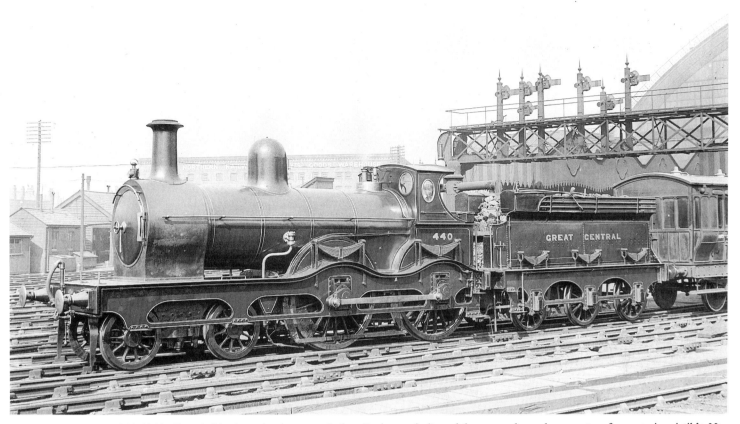

Manchester Central 1901-1912: Though this picture has been seen before, its charm, clarity and sheer panache made a repeat performance irresistible. No. **440**, one of Charles Sacré's Class 6B (LNER D12) engines of 1878, stands outside the station showing off part of the station, signal gantry, the Great Northern's goods warehouse and, of course, its own simple beauty. These charming locomotives appeared under a variety of guises, brought about by various external modifications over the years. Here, No.440 sports an elegant chimney to the design of J.G.Robinson and the whole ensemble, in Great Central passenger green, gleams to perfection. Workings out of Central in the pre-First War era would have taken these splendid engines to Liverpool, on which services they reputedly maintained the 18 minute schedule for the 15¾ miles to Warrington. 440 survived, just, into the post-Grouping years; she was withdrawn (as 440B) in May 1923. *Author's collection*

Manchester Central. c.1930. The station elevation fronting Windmill Street as it appeared in the period between the two World Wars, the only difference being the replacement of the nameboards claiming ownership by the erstwhile Great Northern, Great Central and Midland Railway companies. The covered walkway to the Midland Hotel, seen to the left, was due to be removed as part of the scheme to modernize and concentrate passenger activities in 1951. Like many other proposals it was not completed in its entirety. *Author's collection.*

Manchester Central 19th/20th September 1938: In the Summer of 1938 the LNER organised a travelling exhibition to promote the launch of the new trains for the "Flying Scotsman" service.

On show on that Monday and Tuesday was the famed Stirling Single No. **1**, together with seven 6-wheeled Great Northern coaches, the whole ensemble making up what was described as "The Flying Scotsman of 50 years ago." The highlight of the exhibition was a half-day trip to Liverpool and back by the train on the Wednesday of that week for the princely sum of 3/2d! It is reported that No.1 achieved 65 m.p.h. on the Manchester-Liverpool leg of the journey. Earlier in 1938, in the first week of March, none other than A4 No. **4498** *"Sir Nigel Gresley"* was on show alongside platform 9; possibly the only time an A4 ever entered the precincts.

1) The famous engine stands at platform 8 with its vintage train. Notice the bunting hung especially for the occasion! The onlookers appear to be showing a fair degree of interest, save perhaps for the gentleman with the newspaper who appears somewhat indifferent to the proceedings. Some significance can be put on this occasion by recalling that sights of such historic locomotives were rare in those days. York museum was then very small beer by today's standards, leisure time was much less freely available with the bulk of the population still working a five and a half, or even six, day week   *G.H.Platt*

2) Spending power, too in 1938, was drastically less than today - even the seemingly meagre 3/2d (16p) for the excursion fare would have been a considerable sum to many 54 years ago.

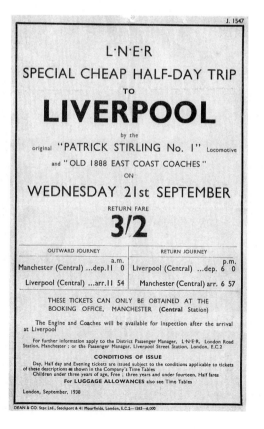

J. 1547

L·N·E·R

SPECIAL CHEAP HALF-DAY TRIP
TO
LIVERPOOL
by the
original "PATRICK STIRLING No. 1" Locomotive
and "OLD 1888 EAST COAST COACHES"
ON
WEDNESDAY 21st SEPTEMBER
RETURN FARE
3/2

OUTWARD JOURNEY	RETURN JOURNEY
a.m.	p.m.
Manchester (Central) ...dep.11 0	Liverpool (Central) ...dep. 6 0
Liverpool (Central) ...arr.11 54	Manchester (Central) arr. 6 57

THESE TICKETS CAN ONLY BE OBTAINED AT THE BOOKING OFFICE, MANCHESTER (**Central** Station)

The Engine and Coaches will be available for inspection after the arrival at Liverpool

For further information apply to the District Passenger Manager, L·N·E·R, London Road Station, Manchester ; or the Passenger Manager, Liverpool Street Station, London, E.C.2

CONDITIONS OF ISSUE
Day, Half day and Evening tickets are issued subject to the conditions applicable to tickets of these descriptions as shown in the Company's Time Tables. Children under three years of age, Free ; three years and under fourteen, Half fares For LUGGAGE ALLOWANCES also see Time Tables

London, September, 1938

DEAN & CO. Stat Ltd., Stockport & 41 Moorfields, London, E.C.2—1583—6,000

LONDON AND NORTH EASTERN RAILWAY

SEE THE

FLYING SCOTSMAN
OF 50 YEARS AGO

ON VIEW AT

MANCHESTER CENTRAL STATION
(No. 9 PLATFORM)
19th & 20th   SEPTEMBER 1938
10-0 a.m. to 6-0 p.m.

ADMISSION FREE

FIFTY YEARS OF SPEED

BRIEF DESCRIPTIVE NOTES OF THE REPLICA TRAIN ON EXHIBITION AND "THE FLYING SCOTSMAN" OF THE PRESENT DAY

3) Taken from the signalbox, the special train is seen leaving Manchester Central for Liverpool at 1.0'clock on Wednesday, 21st. September 1938. Pure vintage stuff; only the colour-light signals and the standard expres headcode date this as a contemporary picture.
Collection of J.M.Bentley

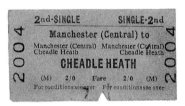

Manchester Central-Approach Viaduct 1951: Like any modern city, Manchester has changed over the years as old buildings have given way to modern developments-changes which, sadly, have not always been for the better. Older readers may recognise the scene here at once, others may need prompting. This is the view looking up to the approach viaduct that fronted onto Whitworth Street West. The water tower seen in some of the station views sprouts up in the centre of the picture, a Stanier 2-6-4 tank waits bunker-first in one of the siding roads. Across in the right-hand corner is Knott Mill and Deansgate station. The "Knott Mill" prefix was dropped in later years, the more prosaic "Deansgate" taking its place. The dilapidated building on the corner of Whitworth Street West and Deansgate was a public house which once rejoiced in the grand name of "The Runcorn, Worsley and Wigan Boat House." In more recent times it was named "The Railway Hotel." At one time there was no through road here down to Deansgate. The nearest thoroughfare was Gaythorn Street which faced the Rochdale Canal. Behind the canal, in between two locks, a large coal and stone yard backed onto Trafford Street which still stands today. The canal enters a tunnel just to the rear of the pub before surfacing again on the other side of Deansgate. Though the Boat House has long gone, nowadays we can see the viaduct in its entirety, restored to pristine condition and refurbished to carry rail-borne traffic once again in the form of "Metrolink." *Author's collection*

Manchester Central-Goods Workings:
i) The Great Eastern-designed J69s formed a small contingent at Trafford Park shed in the 1930s. No. **7198** is viewed across from platform 5 whilst engaged on shunting duties in the station's goods yard. Beyond can be glimpsed wagons standing on the former Great Northern yard, that vast emporium that fronted onto Deansgate and reached, rail-wise, from Great Northern Junction just short of the Castlefield viaducts.
J.M.Bentley collection

ii) Sacre Class 23 0-6-0 of 1866 standing just outside the station goods yard in the early years of the century. The Robinson-style chimney puts the picture as post-1900 but pre-1906 when the engine was withdrawn bearing the duplicate number **219B.** Notice, again, the dominating presence of the G.N. warehouse and the single electric light pendant-then something of a novelty. Central station had become one of the first public buildings in the city to use electric light from around 1898.   *Author's collection*

Manchester Central: That the railways were built prima facie for the transport of goods is, or should be, known to every railway historian. Sadly, this fact never rubbed off on many photographers of the railway scene who tended, for the most part, to concentrate their activities on passenger operations. Something of a rarity, then, is provided by this superb view of Sacre Class 6A 0-6-0 No.**375** standing at the top of the goods yard that was situated alongside the station, between platform 1 and the warehouses along Watson Street. It was on this site that the original terminus opened for traffic in July 1877. No. 375 appears in the dark green livery of the M.S.& L. company. With reddish-brown underframes and white and vermillion lining even the humble goods engine was a sight to behold. Notice the "cab"- a mere weatherboard with no side protection from the elements. 375 had been built at Gorton in 1876 to a design introduced by Sacre two years earlier. She had coupled wheels 5'-3" in diameter and cylinders 17" X 26". Withdrawal took place in 1914. An architectural footnote is provided by the vertical brickwork pillars behind 375's firebox and tender covering the arched girders forming the roof. When the station was rebuilt as "GMEX" the outer brickwork on these pillars was removed in order that the rivetting on the girders could be welded over. Years of neglect and lack of maintenance had wreaked havoc with the station structure and brought it perilously close to the point of collapse.
Author's collection

Manchester Central. December 1947. A new era dawns. One of the pioneer English Electric Co-Co Diesel-Electric locomotives, No.**10000**, pays its first visit to Manchester Central, to be greeted with inquisitive stares. In later years, both No.10000 and its partner, 10001, were quite frquently seen up and down the Midland line on running-in trips from Derby Works.   *P.Ward.*

Manchester Central n.d. : A move to modern times shows us the water tower and turntable roads that provided rudimentary locomotive servicing facilities adjacent to the end of platforms 8 and 9, just above Lower Mosley Street. Former Great Central "Director" No.**62658** *"Prince George"* has backed off the 60 ft. turntable prior to working a stopping passenger train, almost certainly to Chester. Both classes of "Director" saw duty on these trains in their last years as well as attending on station pilot duties. "Prince George" was in the last phase of its life when this picture was taken. It was withdrawn from service in August 1955.   *W.A.Brown*

Manchester Central c.1955: One of the most fascinating workings of modern times in and out of the station were the through Boat Trains from Liverpool to and from the East Coast ports of Harwich and Hull. These had origins going back to the 1880s and, in consequence, had given rise over the years to a very rich variety of both coaching stock and motive power. The usual running arrangement was for the trains to reverse in Manchester Central on both inward and outward legs of the journey. In the mid-1950s the sturdy and dependable Class A5 4-6-2 tanks of the former Great Central were responsible for taking the trains to and from Guide Bridge from where (post-1954) electric traction was used to Sheffield Victoria. On one such occasion A5 No. **69823** stands noisily awaiting departure before running up the Fallowfield line via Fairfield to Guide Bridge. The ex-Great Eastern teak-bodied corridor coach behind the bunker gives the scene a touch of pure vintage.   *W.A.Brown*

Manchester Central 1960: Train watchers in South Manchester had much to interest them in the late 1950s and early '60s. One of the most dynamic of the innovations introduced in those years was certainly the "Midland Pullman." This 6-car Diesel-electric luxury set provided air-conditioned travel between Manchester and St.Pancras (and between there and Leicester via a mid-day service) in the record time of 3 hours, 13 minutes (Up) and 3 hours, 11 minutes (Down). Cheadle Heath was the only stop on both journeys and the train reverted to the old Midland practice of skirting Derby by use of the Chaddesden avoiding line. Completely separate handling of the "Pullman" was undertaken, with stabling and servicing being carried out at Reddish, the depot used for the Manchester-Sheffield electric traction units. (Insert piece about Inspector). This two-tone blue masterpiece is seen underneath the splendid arched roof alongside platform 8 just prior to departure. The train had entered service on July 4th. (a happy coincidence?) 1960. Sadly, it was a short-lived renaissance, the set was withdrawn on inauguration of the onset of the full electrification of the ex-LNWR route in 1966.

Manchester Evening News

THE MIDLAND PULLMAN

THE NECESSITY FOR regular, reliable and quick communication has never been more vital than in the business world of today. The "Midland Pullman" trains, the latest word in luxury, comfort and speed which British Railways are able to offer, have been specially designed with the inter-city travel requirements of the modern businessman principally in mind.

Each morning of the week from Monday to Friday inclusive, starting 4th July 1960, one of these elegant trains in its blue and white livery will leave Manchester and glide easily, smoothly and quickly through some of our most pleasant English countryside to London, returning again to Manchester the same evening.

In the early afternoon it will speed from London to Leicester and back, adding its own lustre to the many existing links between these two great cities.

The name "Pullman" has for long been used in everyday language as a word descriptive of quiet comfort and efficient service of a high standard. The staff of the "Midland Pullman" will be ever-watchful to ensure that these same ideals are maintained and will even try to improve upon them. The trains are equipped to ensure the maximum comfort and well-being of every passenger. The menus will be carefully arranged to tempt the most fickle of palates and a carefully selected wine list will be offered.

The trains are the first of their kind to run on British Railways and are most distinctive in appearance. They have been designed and developed by close teamwork and are the result of much careful thought and planning by the builders, Metropolitan-Cammell Limited, working with the British Transport Commission, the London Midland Region of British Railways and the Pullman Car Company.

The design of the interior of the coaches, the special decor, the fittings and the carpets blend in complete harmony, restful and relaxing

to the traveller. The roomy, individual reclining seats, beautifully cushioned and with comfortable head and arm rests, are of a new design and are adjustable at the touch of a small lever. The main lighting, which is of the fluorescent type, is easy on the eyes and individual lamps are fitted at each table.

In the passenger accommodation, double insulation against sound and heat and double glazing of the windows, incorporating the very latest pattern of fully adjustable venetian blinds between the two panes of glass, are but two of the measures taken to make quite sure the traveller is as comfortable as it is possible to be. In addition, for the first time on any trains in this country, full air conditioning equipment has been installed controlling the temperature and humidity inside the coaches. The gangways between the coaches are of an entirely new type, completely draughtproof and providing insulated connections. Fully suspended floors have also been fitted which will reduce to a minimum any awareness of track vibrations or noise.

Hygiene has been carefully studied in the kitchens, where the most modern types of gas cooker using bottled gas have been installed with a specially large grill capacity for quick service. Constant boiling water is "on tap" and the sterilising sinks are another new feature. Deep freeze equipment together with the normal domestic refrigeration facilities are also provided.

Special attention has been devoted to the toilet accommodation where the temperature of the water can be automatically controlled to individual requirements.

To keep travellers properly informed of the train's progress during their journey, a public address system has been provided.

The trains will each be made up of six coaches (as shown in the diagram) with seating accommodation for a maximum of 132 first class passengers in open type saloons with central gangways. They are powered by two 1,000 h.p. Diesel engine electric generator sets positioned in the power cars, one at each end of the train, next to the driver's compartments. The guard's compartments are also placed in the power cars, between the power units and the passenger accommodation. Two auxiliary power engines for the air conditioning,

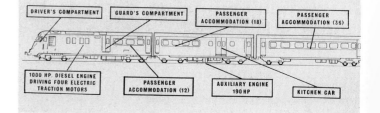

DRIVER'S COMPARTMENT   GUARD'S COMPARTMENT   PASSENGER ACCOMMODATION (18)   PASSENGER ACCOMMODATION (36)

1000 H.P. DIESEL ENGINE DRIVING FOUR ELECTRIC TRACTION MOTORS   PASSENGER ACCOMMODATION (12)   AUXILIARY ENGINE 190HP   KITCHEN CAR

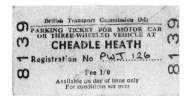

Inside "The Midland Pullman"

lighting, heating and refrigeration, each of 190 h.p., are mounted in the underframes of the auxiliary power and kitchen cars.

As a result of many years of development by the manufacturers a new type of tubular construction has been adopted for the "Midland Pullman" coaches for the first time in this country. Another innovation in the trains is the specially designed draw and buff gear (coupling equipment and the buffers between each coach) which will assist in the smooth "pick-up" of speed by the train on starting and the stable riding of the coaches subsequently. All axles are fitted with roller bearing axleboxes and the Metro-Schlieren bogies are fitted with high speed, two stage air brakes with automatic slack adjusters, and also incorporate helical springs and hydraulic dampers. They will thus play their full part in ensuring the smoothest possible riding of the coaches at speed.

The driver and the guard can communicate with one another through the medium of a Loudaphone installation.

The decorative map on the next two pages illustrates the routes over which the "Midland Pullman" will run and the principal stations through which it will pass. Between Manchester and London the only stop will be at Cheadle Heath. There will be no stops on the afternoon run from London to Leicester and back.

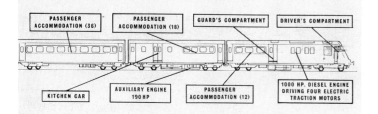

The "Midland Pullman" train, most modern of its kind, provides the fastest regular overland service between Manchester and London.

Details are given below :—

MONDAYS TO FRIDAYS INCLUSIVE FROM 4TH JULY 1960 FIRST CLASS ONLY		
8.50 a.m.	MANCHESTER (Central Station) ↑	9.21 p.m.
9.04 a.m.	Cheadle Heath	9.07 p.m.
12.03 p.m.	LONDON (St. Pancras Station) ↓	6.10 p.m.

PULLMAN CAR SUPPLEMENTARY FEE 20/-

The service between London and Leicester is as follows :—

MONDAYS TO FRIDAYS INCLUSIVE FROM 4TH JULY 1960 FIRST CLASS ONLY		
12.45 p.m.	LONDON (St. Pancras Station) ↑	4.00 p.m.
2.10 p.m.	LEICESTER (London Road Station) ↓	2.33 p.m.

PULLMAN CAR SUPPLEMENTARY FEE 10/-

As the accommodation is limited to 132 seats, passengers should always book in advance to make sure of travelling by this train.

AT A GLANCE...

Maximum speed 90 m.p.h.
Fuel supply for 1,000 mile range
Length of train 409 feet
Weight of train 299 tons ;
power cars $67\frac{1}{4}$ tons ;
parlour cars 33 tons.

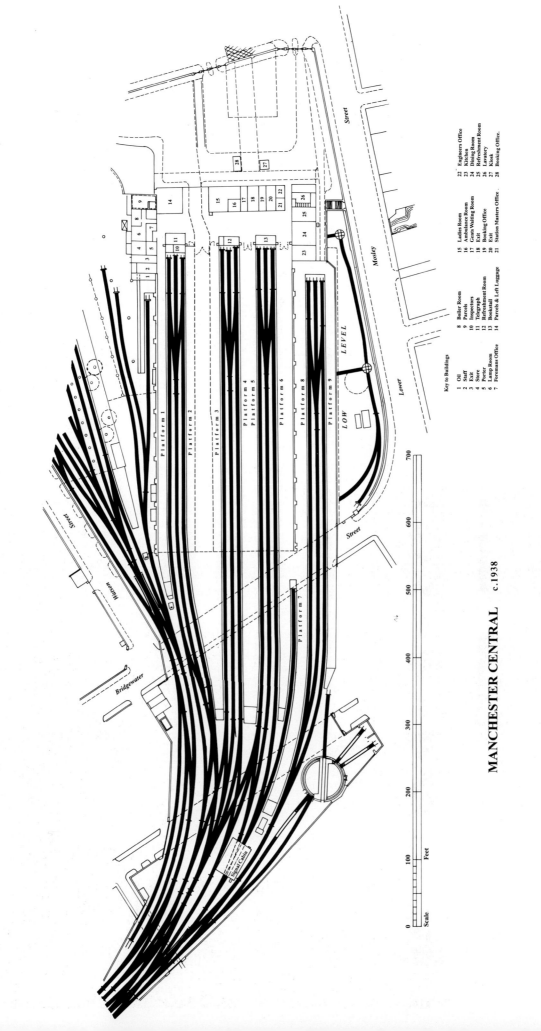

MANCHESTER CENTRAL c.1938

Key to Buildings

1	Oil	8	Boiler Room	15	Ladies Room	22	Engineers Office
2	Staff	9	Parcels	16	Ambulance Room	23	Kitchen
3	Exit	10	Inspectors	17	Gents Waiting Room	24	Dining Room
4	Store	11	Telegraph	18	Exit	25	Refreshment Room
5	Porter	12	Refreshment Room	19	Booking Office	26	Lavatory
6	Lamp Room	13	Bookstall	20	Exit	27	Kiosk
7	Foremans Office	14	Parcels & Left Luggage	21	Station Masters Office	28	Booking Office.

Platform 1
Platform 2
Platform 3
Platform 4
Platform 5
Platform 6
Platform 7
Platform 8
Platform 9

LOW LEVEL

Mosley Street
Lower Street
Bridgewater Street
Watson Street

Signal Cabin

Scale

Feet

0 100 200 300 400 500 600 700

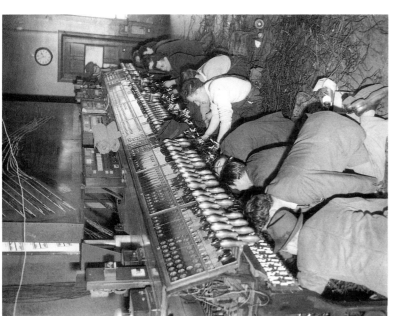

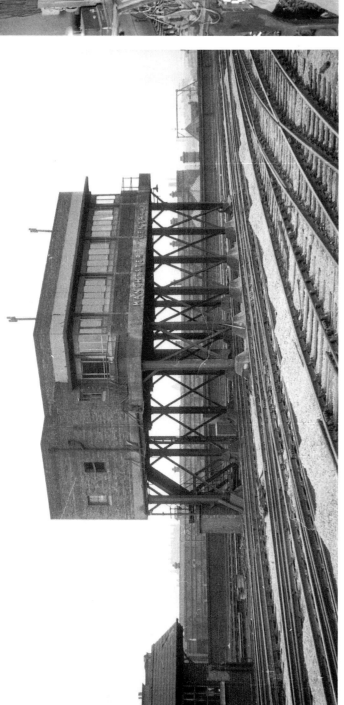

(above left). **Manchester Central Signalbox c.1958:** Apart from motive power changes, one of the most striking differences between the railway scene old and new is the contrast in signalling practice. Not only did lofty semaphores give way to eye-level colour light signals, but signalboxes themselves became fewer in number and, more often than not, architecturally and aesthetically less pleasing. This was the signalbox that controlled all the movements in and out of Manchester Central. The ugly raised brick structure dated from 1935 and, as mentioned, replaced several existing boxes in the vicinity. Taken in the wake of the track re-modelling of 1958, the view looks towards Lower Mosley Street and Whitworth Street West. In the background can be seen the catenary of the M.S.J & A. line to which access could be gained at Cornbrook East Junction.

G.H.Platt

(above). **Manchester Central Signalbox. 1959:** Looking for a moment like one of those pictures where a prize is offered for a suitable caption; this was the scene inside the power signalbox at Manchester Central when the station was finally re-signalled. Anyone who has had the privilege of visiting even a small signalling installation cannot have failed to have been bewildered by the complex array of wiring that attended the numerous track circuits, colour light signals, repeaters and block instruments, to say nothing of the various relays and panel diagrams etc. Something of the mammoth task that faced the S & T engineers and technicians in re-signalling a large installation is provided by this unique view. Notice the new illuminated track circuit panel above the console with the old one just behind.

Harry Bedford

Manchester Central Signalbox Interior, Saturday, May 3rd. 1969: A rare peep inside the nerve centre controlling this once-famous station. Despite being in its death throes, all seems clean, tidy and organised here and not a hint of the impending demise is apparent. Notice, however, the painted-out lines on the signalling diagram: the loco-release road between platforms 1 and 2, together with the goods yard, all the connections to platforms 7, 8 and 9 and the turntable road and associated connections at the back have been removed from traffic. Gone too, is the stabling siding between the "A" and "B" roads further down near to Cornbrook West Junction.

G.H.Platt

Manchester Central Sunday, April 27th.1969: Surprisingly few pictures exist showing the full width of the interior of the train shed with its splendid 210 ft single span. This is one of them, taken at 10.25 in the morning on Sunday April 27th. 1969 when the station had just one week of life left. Diesel-Multiple units occupy platforms 4 and 5 now, for steam has long gone from the railway network. It seems strange that the newer forms of motive power were unable to save the South District line local services-though DMUs were used on the Buxton trains for a period. Under phase 4 of the Woodhead electrification scheme of 1954 it had been intended to bring the catenary down to include the Fairfield line services via Chorlton Junction. In the event, the Overhead only ever got as far as Reddish, financial constraints, as ever, prohibiting the extension of what was a splendid idea.   *W.J.Skillern*

Manchester Central March 30th. 1966: Diesel locomotives were no strangers to South District line services, both Semi-Fast and Express workings had seen this form of motive power since the LMS had first conceived the Diesel-Electric genre for main-line working in late 1947. The well-known and successful 1 Co-Co 1 Type 4 or "Peaks" first appeared on the St.Pancras expresses in the Autumn of 1958. Here **D82**, carrying the headcode 2P 53, waits to leave platform 3 with the 8-coach 7.30 a.m. all stations to Derby. The wisp of steam would have been issuing from the train heating boiler, giving overtones of times past. The plain edge to the valance of the platform canopy makes an interesting comparison with the pre-Grouping pictures.   *Peter.E.Baughan*

Manchester Central, the Great Northern's Deansgate Engine Shed c.1958:
The Great Northern company had set great store on Manchester as a potential source of traffic. Their new goods warehouse adjacent to Central Station and opened in 1898 was provided with its own engine shed; this notwithstanding the G.N's joint ownership of the Trafford Park depot with the G.C. and the Midland. Seen here from the approaches to Central, the engine shed, complete with water tank on top, stood hard by Great Northern Junction above Collier Street where the warehouse line forked away from the running lines. Never used for the purpose for which it was built, the shed did duty as a wagon repair shop before falling into disuse. Notice the remodelled trackwork with the junction to the warehouse site now severed.

G.H.Platt

Manchester central. 10th April 1958.
Throughout much of 1958 and well into 1959, extensive engineering and signalling work was undertaken at the approaches to Manchester Central Station. Briefly, it involved the elimination of sharp curves, the installation of colour light signalling and lengthening of platforms. According to contemporary reports, some three miles of track, including 46 switches and 77 crossings were replaced. Signalling alterations included replacement of two gantries by a single unit with a span of 65 feet. It was anticipated that work would be completed by June 1959 although some trains that normally ran into London Road would use Central for a time whilst electrification work at the former was taking place. This view shows some of the remodelling at an early stage to the east of Cornbrook Viaduct.

British Railways.

Manchester Central. October 1967.
Much of the remodelling mentioned above had a relatively short life, given that Central was to close in May 1969. This view west across Cornbrook Viaduct from the carriage of a St.Pancras bound train shows a layout which these days would be considered far too complex and costly. *M.S. Welch.*

There were two pairs of running lines between Manchester Central and Throstle Nest East Junction where the Liverpool and South District lines parted company. They were referred to as Up and Down "A" and Up and Down "B"; they ran roughly east (Up) and west (Down). Until 1958 they were joined by the line from the Deansgate goods yard. It is worth noting that the "Up" lines at this point ran into the station (from Liverpool). From Throstle Nest East the South District lines became the more normal "Up" and "Down" again-to and from London.

The Down lines from Manchester Central lay on a continuously falling grade of 1 in 70 to 1 in 132. At Cornbrook West Junction they took an easy curve to the right; connections from the Altrincham line came sweeping in here from the left, just in front of the signalbox. The distance between Manchester Central and Cornbrook West was approximately 1¼ miles and between there and Throstle Nest East was about ¼ mile. Throstle Nest East received its name upon the opening of the 1906 line from Throstle Nest South Junction round to Trafford Park sidings. Prior to that it was known as plain "Throstle Nest Junction." Opposite Cornbrook West box there was a stabling siding between the "A" and the "B" lines. The most significant feature of the railway scene hereabouts were the extensive carriage sidings at Cornbrook which were sited in front of the West Junction signalbox behind the main lines and backing onto Chester Road.

After parting company with the Liverpool line at Throstle Nest East Junction, the South District line curved away to the left to yet another junction-this time Throstle Nest South from where a sharp curve ran round to parallel the Liverpool line which it joined at Trafford Park Junction to gain access to the previously-mentioned siding complex. For those with a bent for the unusual the name "Throstle" is an old English word denoting a Thrush. Throstle Nest Lane in Old Trafford together, with a local pub, "The Throstle Nest Hotel, perpetuates the quaintly-named junctions.

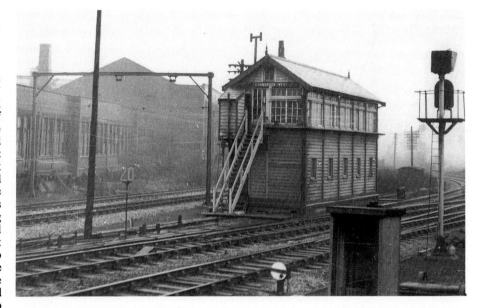

Cornbrook Junction. February 1968.
The two junctions at Cornbrook provided a facility whereby traffic from the two main lines out of Manchester Central, the South District and the Liverpool, were able to cross the M.S.J. & A. (Altrincham) line and vice-versa. This view was taken from the rear of a DMU travelling into Manchester Central and shows quite clearly the three pairs of running lines. On the extreme left is the MSJ&A line, identified by the overhead catenary. Just behind here was the first part of the complex designated Cornbrook East Junction. The box here was situated on the Altrincham line and handled traffic to and from Oxford Road. Ahead is Cornbrook West signal box controlling the junction of the same name; the tall splitting homes relate to the fork ahead at this junction - left to gain access to Cornbrook carriage sidings and the Manchester Ship Canal system before rejoining the Altrincham line at Old Trafford Junction and straight on to Throstle Nest East. The middle pair of lines are the Up and Down 'A' lines, whilst off to the right are the respective 'B' lines.   *G.H. Platt.*

Cornbrook West Junction. c.1968.
Signal boxes close to city termini seem to ave been rarely photographed, lack of pedestrian access being a major obstacle. This view of Cornbrook West Junction was taken from a tain passing along the Down Liverpool line (Down 'B' line). In the background are the lines of the MSJ&A whilst in front of the box are the Up and Down 'A' lines leading to Throstle Nest East Junction, dividing point of the Derby/Liverpool lines. Just visible on the far right is the junction giving access to the extensive Cornbrook Carriage Sidings and leading also to Old Trafford Junction to regain the MSJ&A.
                    G.H. Platt.

Old Trafford Junction n.d: Access to the siding complex at Cornbrook and that of the Manchester Ship Canal could be obtained at Cornbrook West Junction. From here a spur led down to Old Trafford Junction where traffic joined the M.S.J.& A. system. This was the route followed by the Manchester Central-Chester trains and was also used in the early 1960s as a diversionary route for Manchester-London trains; starting from Manchester Central, these travelled as far as Northwich on the Chester line before taking the route to Sandbach where the Crewe line was encountered for the rest of the trip. Such a journey is in prospect for "Jubilee" No.**45583** *Assam* as she comes off the curve from Cornbrook West and goes "under the wire" to travel down towards Altrincham. The building at the top of the cutting was an electric sub-station station providing current at 1500 v. dc for the "overhead" on the Altrincham line. *T.Lewis*

Throstle Nest South Junction, 1965: Rarely photographed, Throstle Nest South Junction lay in a shallow cutting behind Chester Road and alongside Boyer Street. Here a very sharp curve, notice the speed restriction board and check rail, enabled trains from the South District line to gain access to the Liverpool line, so avoiding Manchester Central. The box housed a 24-lever frame and was quite a busy place. Perusal of the train register for Thursday, September 26th. 1957 shows 70 trains passing on the Up line and 67 on the Down. Signalmen manning the box at Throstle Nest South in that period were A.W.Wood, J.Barry, K.Eyres, H.Thompson, J.Tysling and W.Watson. Diligently recorded are the destinations of all the trains that passed by: a sample for September 27th. records Cheadle, Buxton, London, Derby, Guide Bridge, Sheffield, Newton Heath, Hull, Nottingham, Harwich and Leicester. Entries such as "E.R.Fish", "Derby Parcels" and "Mail" prove a busy system still handling traffic that has, by and large, slipped away. Throstle Nest South Junction was re-named "Throstle Nest Junction" upon the closure of Central station. Thereafter, the connections to and from the Central Station side of the junction were removed. The box was finally abolished on Sunday, April 5th. 1970. Under stage II of the extension of the London Road (not, note, "Piccadilly") power box scheme, just two signals and three track circuits took its place. *G.H.Platt*

Trafford Park Junction 1930: From the main line the junction to the running shed and Trafford Park sidings turns off to the right whilst the Liverpool line runs ahead towards Trafford Park station. Here, the signalbox is on our left; the far track on that side of the picture is a spur which joined the Down line 19 chains further on. The two main running lines (Up to Manchester Central) form the middle pair; to the right is the line that served the United F.C.Halt situated in front of the boarded fence.   *G.H.Platt*

Trafford Park Junction May 1969: An opposite view, taken from a train running towards Manchester Central on the Up line. Ahead is Throstle Nest East Junction which takes the Derby line round to Throstle Nest South. In front of the junction home signals can just be seen the connections bringing the two tracks round from Throstle Nest South to join the Liverpool line. This is the section dating from 1906; the alignment here was widened to accommodate the two extra tracks. At the same time the signalbox site was moved from the opposite side of the line to produce this all-timber structure.   The box carries a nameboard of standard CLC design, the small upper window owes something to Great Central practice. Behind the signalbox runs Railway Road, Stretford, whilst opposite (though out of sight) is the football ground of the legendary Manchester United-situated in Old Trafford. Behind the United Football ground was the vast, sprawling dock empire of the Manchester Ship Canal with its own railway system-much of it sited in the City of Salford. *G.H.Platt*

Trafford Park Junction, 1930: A view inside the box showing off the 57-lever frame to advantage: a surprisingly sharp picture considering the difficulty of photographing such subjects. The frame is to the CLC's own design; a development of the Stevens Tappet frame; the CLC produced their own lever frames and other signalling apparatus at their Warrington signal works. The six accepting block instruments-controlling the various sections from Trafford Park station, Trafford Park sidings, Throstle Nest East and Throstle Nest South junctions are ranged over the block shelf. The sloping board at the far end of the lever frame was to give assistance when pulling off the down distant-the extra bit of purchase was always welcome for such problems. Trafford Park Junction was still lit by oil lamps when this picture was taken.
G.H.Platt

Trafford Park Junction. 1939. Shortly before the outbreak of W.W.2, LNER 4-4-2T Class C14 No.**6121** was seen passing the Old Trafford home of Manchester United F.C. with an eight coach local train. Apparently, these locomotives were not frequently to be seen on the Liverpool line, although if trains this length were the order of the day, it is hardly surprising. Twelve locomotives made up the class, all built for the Great Central Railway by Beyer, Peacock in 1907. Having served three owners in her lifetime, No 6121 was withdrawn as British Railways No.67441 in August 1957. The single platform station serving the football ground can be seen beyond the rear of the train. *W.Potter.*

Trafford Park Shed

It was from Trafford Park Shed, situated on the north side of the Liverpool line, that most of the motive power for services out of Manchester Central emanated. Upon the opening of a station at Central in 1877, locomotive stabling facilities had been provided at Cornbrook alongside the Bridgewater Canal. This was a fairly simple 3-road shed sited hard by the running lines. At Trafford Park, the Midland Railway shared joint tenure with the Great Central and, from 1898, the Great Northern. Opened in March, 1895, "TP", as it was known to us Manchester spotters in the 1950s, was accessed from Trafford Park Junction. Under joint LMS and LNE ownership after the Grouping, the 20-road running shed was spanned by seven hipped roof sections; later photographs show these to be in a state of dire neglect which was never totally remedied. The depot had a fascinating number of allocation codes. It began life as Midland shed 21A (a sub-shed of Belle Vue). The Great Northern coded it as No.7. The LMS used the code 19G-actually an outpost of Sheffield, but under the day-to-day supervision of Longsight. Under BR authority it became 13A-a district in itself. This lasted but briefly when, later in 1950, it became 9E and was under Longsight authority again. From January 1957 until April 1958 it suffered yet another change of ownership when it became a subject of the Derby empire and was coded 17F. Finally allocated code 9E, Trafford Park shed remained intact almost until the end of steam and almost as long as Manchester Central itself. It was closed completely on March 4th. 1968. The site is now covered by a Freightliner depot.

Trafford Park, c.1959: Something of a revolution in locomtive power occured in the early summer of 1958 when six "Britannia" Pacifics arrived to work the St.Pancras-Manchester expresses. For years nothing bigger than "Jubilees" had plied the route and it has to be said that, often, their time-keeping was deplorable. **70017** *Arrow* was transferred from Cardiff (Canton) to Trafford Park and became a firm favourite with my little circle of teenage spotters. We always rated Trafford Park as an "easy" shed as access was liberal and we seemed in complete freedom to roam around. In the background can be seen one the repaired roof sections. Something of a contrast to the 4F view! *W.A.Brown*

Trafford Park 1930s: Showing well the hipped roof construction of the shed, former Great Central Class 8G (LNER B9) No.**6111** shows off her stately proportions, a note from the whistle and a well-coaled tender indicating a readiness for work. Built solely for goods work, the LNER employed these engines for a time in hauling traffic out of the Deansgate goods warehouse.

G.H.Platt

Trafford Park, May 12th. 1951: This now roofless section of the shed is typical of many railway buildings of the period at a time when bureaucracy was top-heavy and investment was low. The ubiquitous 4F, this one being an example from the LMS-built series No.**44555**, needs no introduction. Though perhaps a comment might be made that these far-flung and hard-worked engines weren't, perhaps, quite the duffers some writers have made them out to be. *B.K.B.Green*

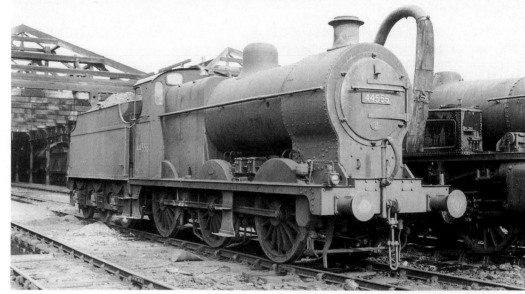

Trafford Park, c.1955: We viewed one of J.G.Robinson's original "Directors"-11E over at Manchester Central and no apologies are offered for another picture of one of these superb 4-4-0s. This is one of the second series of these famous engines (G.C.11F) No.**62670** *Marne* built at Gorton in December 1922 at the very end of the Great Central's existence as a separate entity. 62670 stands at the far right of the shed, at the south end adjacent to the offices and stores. At this time the "Directors" were working out of Central on stopping trains to Chester along the old MSJ&A and CLC route via Altrincham and Knutsford. Despite having been out-shopped from Gorton Works devoid of lining and with a blank tender (!), *"Marne"* still carries that certain dignity; a stateliness still apparent even when performing such mundane duties as station pilot at Manchester Central in the mid-'50s. *B.K.B.Green*

An Act dated July 25th.1890 gave consent for a railway to leave the South District line between Chorlton-cum-Hardy and Old Trafford, tunnel beneath the site of the future Lancashire County Cricket ground (shades of the Great Central!) and over the C.L.C. main line to Liverpool. At this point access to the Manchester Ship Canal's system at Trafford Wharf would have been obtained. In the event, the railway was never built; the nearest connection to the M.S.C's rail network being the 1906 curve from Throstle Nest South to

Trafford Park Junction. It was, almost certainly, the possibility of this connection being established that led to the fascinating little signal box described here being built.

Seymour Road, September 1991: Perhaps this picture would be more at home in a book on wild flowers. This is milepost 2, just north of where Seymour Road box was situated. A standard CLC artefact, "M" stood for "Main", the 2 miles being the distance from Manchester Central. Painted white, with black lettering and base, this would appear to be one of the very few relics of railway life left on the line today. *Author*

Seymour Road, 1928: Between Throstle Nest South Junction and Chorlton-cum-Hardy was the block post known as Seymour Road. Opened c.1892, the box was situated in Old Trafford and was sited between the overbridges taking Kings Road (bridge No.7) and Ayres Road (bridge No. 6) over the railway. Seymour Road housed a 12-lever frame and controlled a crossover road and signals for both running lines. The name of the box was somewhat at odds with the locality as there was no thoroughfare in the vicinity that bore the name "Seymour Road"; the nearest applicable name was "Seymour Grove", a main road in the area. Seymour Road signalbox was closed in September 1928 and its function replaced by Intermediate Block signals: a Down I.B.S. 916 yards from Chorlton Station box, and an Up IBS 1030 yards from Throstle Nest South Junction box. Our view shows one of the L&Y 2-4-2 tanks, No.**10901**, just clearing Kings Road with an Up Local train in 1928. The 2-4-2s were transferred to Trafford Park in 1926 to work South District line Local trains. Natty little engines, they replaced the Deeley 0-6-4 tanks and remained, as far as is known, before being gradually supplanted by new Fowler 2-6-4 tank engines from late 1929 onwards. *G.H.Platt*

Chorlton-cum-Hardy, Manchester Road, c.1938: J39 No.**1298** passes under the Manchester Road bridge just outside Chorlton-cum-Hardy station with the 8.22 p.m. Up Deansgate to Colwick Fitted Goods. This appears to be one of the very few photographs of trains ex-Deansgate Goods yard running over this section of the South District line. The train, together with the 8.30 p.m. Kings Cross to Deansgate, travelled over a route first used in 1899 to ward off the obstructionist tactics of the Great Central. The route followed the Midland's Dore and Chinley and Erewash Valley lines to Codnor Park Junction before taking the 55-chain G.N.branch to Brinsley Junction and on over G.N. metals to Colwick (Nottingham). The Colwick goods was manned by a Trafford Park crew who returned to Manchester on the Down train which left Colwick at 12.42 a.m. The service continued to operate over the CLC/Midland route until September 1952. Then, with the closing of the G.N. Brinsley spur line, the train was diverted to run over Woodhead.

Chorlton-cum-Hardy, 1955: From their inception in 1900, the Midland Compounds, together with their later LMS counterparts, had been regular performers over the South District line on both express, semi-fast and stopping passenger trains. Here, No. **41066**-one of the LMS engines built in 1924, puts up a good performance as she enters Chorlton station with an Up express. 41066 was withdrawn in May 1958.

W.Johnson

Chorlton-cum-Hardy, c.1951: Ex-Great Central J10 0-6-0 No.**65179** runs into Chorlton station with the daily pick-up or "Pilot" goods. Little has altered in either motive power, operation, or infrastructure here since the late years of the last century. Notice the slewed arrangement of the goods yard headshunt, effected when the platforms were lengthened in 1889. This section of railway became CLC territory as far as Chorlton Junction in 1891, a fact marked out by the distinctive signalbox (named "Chorlton Station") and the characteristic and very prominent Down Home signal. The signalbox replaced a Midland-pattern structure that stood on the same site.

N.F.W.Dyckhoff

Chorlton-cum-Hardy, January 1st.1967: A scene looking towards Chorlton Junction on the last day of the station's existence. An interesting contrast in architectural styles presented itself at Chorlton: the buildings on the Down (right-hand) side were very evidently Midland: the platform canopy was added in 1884 at a cost of £975. The buildings on the opposite (Up) side were more akin to typical Cheshire Lines practice and were added after the CLC had assumed responsibility for the line upon the opening of the Manchester Central Station Railway. Sadly now, this CLC-style structure looks very care-worn and neglected. Surprisingly, long after closure, in 1985/86, the remaining platform (on the Up side) was cut back to accommodate 8'-6" wide containers, an example of one of numerous routes cleared for the passage of such vehicles.

W.A.Brown

Chorlton-cum-Hardy, c.1913: Pure vintage stuff is this splendid summer scene showing one of the Great Central's celebrated "Sir Sam Fay" 4-6-0s about to enter the station with the 3.20 p.m. Continental Boat Express ex-Manchester Central. The train began its journey in Liverpool at 2.30 and was due into Sheffield at 4.27. Here the train divided; one portion going on to Harwich which was reached at 9.35-the other via Barnetby and Brocklesby to arrive at Grimsby (Town) at 7.08 and Cleethorpes at 7.23.
Collection of Alan Wilkinson

Chorlton-cum-Hardy, Summer 1959: Along with West Didsbury, Didsbury and Heaton Mersey, the station here had opened for passengers on January 1st.1880. A rather different architectural style pervaded at Chorlton, one that was reflected further along the line at Heaton Mersey. A footbridge spanning the tracks had been provided here in 1884, but no usable pictures of it survive. The ramp from which the photograph was taken was also added in the same year at a cost of £47; the through road in the village was known in those days as "Princes Road" and became Wilbraham Road later on. When London Docklands-style plastic "buildings" nowadays pass for station accommodation, one can only marvel at the beautifully-inlaid brickwork, elaborate fretted bargeboards and cast-iron ridge pieces; all passed into history now. The Safeway supermarket development, built hard by the Down line, has long since obliterated such finery.
E.M.Johnson

Chorlton-cum-Hardy, March 1960: A bare winter landscape of barren trees forms a back-drop to this scene as "Britannia" Pacific No.**70014** *Iron Duke* roars into the station with the 2.25 p.m. from Manchester Central to St.Pancras. Named "The Palatine", this express revived a title first introduced by the LMS in 1938. Giving a 3 hour, 45 minute journey time between the two cities in the Up direction, "The Palatine" was the only named express to ply this route in the post-War period. Sadly, such frivolities are but a memory in today's anonymous Inter-City network. Notice the platform extension on this, the Up side of the line. Each platform had been extended at both ends in late 1889 at a cost of £168, work requiring the re-alignment of the headshunt in the goods yard.   *W.A.Brown*

Chorlton-cum-Hardy c.1927: As mentioned in the Central Station feature, the Deeley "Flatiron" 0-6-4 tanks were something of a mainstay as far as South District line local services were concerned. No.**2002** is seen passing under the Wilbraham Road overbridge leaving Chorlton station with an Up local in the 1920s. The carriages are comprised of the Midland 48 ft. close-coupled sets to a design by David Bain. This stock, built especially for these services in 1903, ran in sets of nine and was gas-lit when built. Modellers may like to take note that the footboards from this stock were removed from around 1930; several examples from the sets survived Nationalisation.   *G.H.Platt*

Chorlton-cum-Hardy c. Autumn 1926: One of the few photographs of the famous Beyer-Ljüngström condensing-turbine locomotive in traffic. Built at the famous Beyer, Peacock Gorton Foundry in the summer of 1926, this peculiar-looking machine was first put into service between Gorton and Woodhead on the 4th. of July that year. It was later tried out on Derby-Manchester slow and semi-fast passenger workings in the latter part of 1926 having been completed in the summer of that year. Later, in May 1927, it was tried on express services between Derby and Manchester. The 73 ft.11 in., 143 ton locomotive is seen here approaching Chorlton station with a down train in what is believed to be its first period of working. The rolling stock consists of four carriages belonging to a South District close-coupled set with several goods vans at the rear. Like so many attempts to improve the thermal efficiency of the steam locomotive, the Ljungström engine met with mixed success. A building cost of around £37,000 compared with some £6,000 for a conventional reciprocating locomotive was more than enough to outweigh any savings that might have been incurred. The Ljungström engine remained stored out of use at Gorton until 1940; thereafter, its boiler found service as a stationary steam supplier to the boiler shop there.   *N.Fields*

Chorlton Junction

Just south of the station at Chorlton-cum-Hardy was Chorlton Junction. Here the Midland's South District line was met by the Great Central's (erstwhile M.S.& L.) line from Fairfield. The latter had opened to Fallowfield on October 1st. 1891 and from there to Fairfield on May 2nd. 1892. The opening of the first section had particular significance for the railway here, as from that date ownership of the South District as far as Throstle Nest Junction (later on Throstle Nest East) passed into the hands of the C.L.C.

Chorlton Junction c.1926/27: No. **10902**, one of the little Lancashire & Yorkshire Railway 2-4-2 tanks that worked South District local trains in the period 1926-30 approaches Chorlton Junction with an Up train. The coaching stock consists of one of the 9-coach close-coupled suburban sets referred to earlier.
G.H.Platt

Chorlton Junction, 1921: A Midland Railway Compound, No. **1011** of 1906, is seen at the head of the 6.25 p.m. (Sunday) Manchester Central to St.Pancras express. Together with its train of square-panelled clerestory stock, the locomotive presents something of a "classic" Midland scene and provides an interesting contrast with later views. The lofty Cheshire Lines-pattern semaphores carry a curious demarcation: the taller arm, pegged "off" for the train, carries a Midland-pattern finial; the post for the branch is topped by a CLC finial-a shape of an altogether different type. In later years the CLC won the day for both posts. Modellers beware! The signal lasted until the late 1950s.
G.M.Shoults

Chorlton Junction, c.1920/21: Providing evidence of the alternative route to the Capital out of Manchester Central we are able to glimpse the Great Central's service to London (Marylebone) by way of this view of No. **426** *City of Chester*. Taken at almost exactly the same spot as No. 1011, this is the 5.15 p.m. (Sunday) Manchester Central to Marylebone. Travelling over the notorious Woodhead route, the Great Central's express timings between Manchester and London ran to just under 5 hours in those days. 1011 and its Midland train completed the run to St.Pancras in just under 4 1/2 hours. *G.M.Shoults*

Chorlton Junction n.d: Two of the final three Fowler 2-6-4 tanks were transferred to Trafford Park in November, 1929 after spending a brief spell at Manningham (Bradford). On an evidently sunny day No. **2373** bursts under the St.Werburgh's Road overbridge at the head of another one of the 9-coach close-coupled carriage sets (notice the footboards are now removed.) The new brickwork of the bridge will be noted, the structure was renewed around 1927/28 to provide accommodation for a widened road and what appeared to be the possibility of a quadrupled line. The bridge stands to this day and though now entirely bereft of trackwork, the blackened remains of the original structure can still be seen on the Down (left-hand) side set inside the later brickwork. *G.M.Shoults*

Chorlton Junction, 1929: A most interesting picture, taken from the signalbox, showing bridge No.16, 3 miles, 43 chains from Manchester Central, in the course of rebuilding. Carrying St.Werburgh's Road over the railway this bridge, as mentioned elsewhere, was widened to accommodate quadrupled track. Class C1 GN Atlantic No.**4428** swings off the South District line and heads up towards Wilbraham Road with a cross-country express-possibly the 11.22 a.m. from Manchester Central to Barnetby (and beyond). To the side of the line, the contractor's plant is arrayed in working order as the new bridge abutments rise from the ground. A little bit of social history is provided by the sight of the Manchester Billposting Company's hoarding proclaiming attractions at the Kingsway Super Cinema. On offer is Richard Dix in "Easy Come Easy Go", and Syd Chaplin in "Charley's Aunt." Names still with us are also seen: Threlfalls Ales, Ewbank (The British Carpet Sweeper) and the ever-famous Bovril-"saved my life again." All visible in a quick glimpse by passengers en route through here to all corners of the Kingdom.   *G.H.Platt*

Chorlton Junction c.1921: One of a fascinating trio of pictures taken by Mr.G.M.Shoults showing the signalbox at Chorlton Junction in the immediate pre-Grouping period. An all-timber structure, the box was a typically Midland period II design. Reference to CLC practice, however, is provided by the ventilator and nameboard-both standard items of that concern. An interesting reflection proving the joint nature of the box related to the three different patterns of block instruments here: CLC pattern for the section down to Chorlton Station, Great Central for the section to Alexandra Park (later Wilbraham Road) and Midland for the section to Withington and West Didsbury.   *G.M.Shoults*

Chorlton Junction, May 29th. 1951: Viewed from the signalbox window is the 4-coach 5.05 p.m. from Rotherham (West) to Manchester Central drawn by Class 2 4-4-0 No.**40487**. The sweeping curve of the branch up to Wilbraham Road swings away to the left.   *R.E.Gee*

Chorlton Junction, July 1961 : Drawn by a "Peak" Class Diesel (then designated Type "4"), an Up special working from Derby to Manchester Central via Stockport Tiviot Dale speeds over the junction on a fine summer evening. Although they were later abandoned, the 4-character headcodes-in this case "2H 53"-provided a useful means of identifying trains for those enthusiasts privy to a working timetable.   *E.M.Johnson*

Chorlton Junction c.1927: Off for a day out is LNER B7 4-6-0 No. **5476** heading an Up excursion over onto the Fallowfield line, up through Fairfield to Guide Bridge and then over Woodhead to Sheffield and, probably, the East Coast. Of interest is the original overbridge in the background and the ramshackle farm buildings along the lineside. An incredible-looking telegraph pole sprouts from the smokebox of the locomotive!   *G.H.Platt*

Around the time after the First War much of the land between Chorlton Junction and Heaton Mersey was still occupied by farms, the great Manchester urban sprawl having yet to spread its tentacles. Just south of Chorlton Junction ran a straight length of railway which seems to have attracted the interest of quite a few photographers.

South of Chorlton Junction. 1900. Very few pictures of Midland trains on the South District appear to have survived, so it was a particular joy to stumble across this superb view of the 10.30am Manchester Central to St.Pancras Dining Car Express clearing the junction at (to quote) "50 Miles an Hour". Taken from the long defunct magazine "Locomotives and Railways" the illustration shows a Johnson 4-4-0 in typically spanking condition at the head of a 5-coach train. The number of the engine is unknown, but we can deduce that it is one of the later series of S.W. Johnson's superbly-proportioned designs, possibly one of the "150" Class with piston valves above the cylinders. This, surely, was the Victorian railway scene at its very pinnacle; the acme of perfection.
Author's collection

South of Chorlton Junction c.1927: The double-heading of Midland trains is something which has passed into the realms of railway folklore. Even into modern times this practice was still common, and was related in the Introduction. Here, just past the junction, a rebuilt Class 2 and a Compound crack along with an Up express. Although the make-up of the somewhat mixed train cannot be accurately described, an LNWR-liveried carriage appears to have found its way behind the train engine's tender! *G.H.Platt*

South of Chorlton Junction c.1922: A truly atmospheric scene as Class 2 4-4-0 No. **433** pulls away from the junction with an Up express. The train comprises five clerestory carriages and an arc-roofed vehicle behind the tender. Chorlton Junction is now in the background; the splitting homes can just be glimpsed. The tall semaphores protecting the branch to Fairfield make an interesting comparison with those seen in the earlier view of the Rotherham train. *G.M.Shoults*

South of Chorlton Junction, n.d: Former Midland Class 2 4-4-0 No.**461** strides away from the junction with an Up stopping train. Notice, in the background, the widened bridge referred to in an adjacent caption.   *W.Lees*

South of Chorlton Junction, n.d: Prior to around 1939 Stanier Class 5 4-6-0s were the largest engines permitted to work north of Derby into Manchester, a prohibition due to deficiencies in certain bridges in the Chapel-en-le-Frith area. On an unknown date, Class 5 No.**5040** heads south with a six-coach express. A brake third plus and all-third form the first part of the train with a 12-wheel Stanier Restaurant Car behind. The fourth vehicle is a square-windowed LMS carriage with two Stanier vehicles bringing up the rear.   *W.Lees*

South of Chorlton Junction, February 1938: LMS Compound No.**936** speeds down towards the junction with an express from Nottingham. The tender paired to this locomotive was a standard Fowler type which had been rebuilt with the high curved sides, seen here, in May 1933. Originally fitted to 4F No.4453, it remained with No.936 until 1954. Notice the open aspect of the landscape here, still, thankfully, evident today. In the background can be seen the bridge carrying Mauldeth Road West over the railway. Numbered 21, it was re-constructed in 1927, having originally carried the name of "Hough End Clough." Along with the bridges at Chorlton Junction, Princess Road, Parr's Wood Road and Kingsway it was provided with a span sufficient for quadruple track-in this case 59'-3" on the skew. Were four tracks were planned or not; or were the widened bridges simply a contingency? The wooden steps at the side were numbered 21A; designated "timber stepway"- they were directed to be maintained by Manchester Corporation.   *W.Lees*

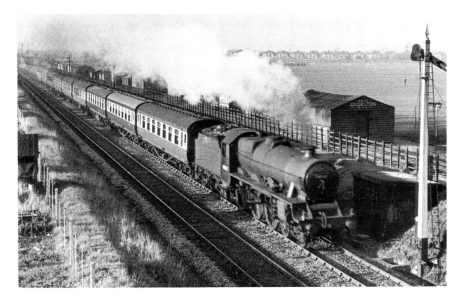

Withington

Officialdom never seemed certain as to what title suited the station at Withington best. Though actually situated in West Didsbury and sited something like a mile from the village proper of Withington, the station upheld something of a tongue-in-cheek attitude by the railway companies when it came to giving stations a name that actually matched their true location. Opening on January 1st. 1880 Withington's station first bore the title of plain "Withington." Realising that the fashionable housing development at nearby Albert Park was worth courting for passenger traffic, the Midland Railway changed the station's name to "Withington and Albert Park" on July 1st. 1884. This lasted until April 1st. 1915 when the name was changed yet again; this time to "Withington and West Didsbury", the title carried until closure on July 3rd. 1961.

Just after the turn of the century, Manchester's electric trams began to run from the adjacent West Didsbury terminus into the heart of the city and were doubtless responsible for bleeding away much of the abundant passenger traffic from the railway. Looking back at passenger receipts on the South District line it is hard to believe that the decline began as far back as 1901. No less than 233,922 passenger bookings were made through the station in 1900; significantly, the electric tramcars had begun service at the end of 1902.

Hough End Fields, c.1951: Taken on the south side of bridge No.21 here we look from Princess Road towards Chorlton Junction, roughly half-way between there and West Didsbury. Coming up the line is "Jubilee" No.**45557** *New Brunswick* with a 9-coach Up express. The signal is the West Didsbury Up Outer Distant-a hardy specimen which lasted almost until the line closed. Allotments face on to the track on the Down side; over on the Up side was the home of Chorlton A.F.C. It was not unknown for spectators to have their attention diverted at moments like this! *N.F.W.Dvckhoff*

The glory that once was Rome-Withington and Albert Park, c.1900: Epitomising the peak of Midland Railway practice around the turn of the century is this view of an Up express hauled by two Johnson 4-4-0s, still in original condition, passing Withington's signalbox. All seems well in the world here as the signalman glances at the photographer, the sun shines down on the crimson lake and polished brass of the two engines, and the telegraph boards shows "all right." The box seen here dated from the opening of the line in 1880. A typical Midland period 1 signalbox, it possesses the high-waisted timber panelling characteristic of the early style of Midland box. *Collection of J.Braithwaite*

Withington and Albert Park 1880s: One of S.W.Johnson's superb-looking "1500" Class 2-4-0 locomotives, No.**1521**, viewed standing at the end of the Down platform. The rather cumbersome-looking pipework projecting from the smokebox is part of the Smith simple vacuum brake-a device used by the Midland at this time as well as the M.S.& L. Modellers take note also that the letters "MR" have yet to appear on the tender side and also that this lacks coal rails. Also on show here are contemporary Midland station uniforms: the frock-coated gentleman in the "six-foot" is the Stationmaster whilst the guard poses with hands on the loco and tender handrails. Behind are the loco crew, the Driver resting his hands on the reversing screw. Some features of the trackwork make for interesting reading: Midland track at this time was laid with rail in 30' lengths and weighed 85 lb. per yard. As is clearly visible, the chairs were fitted with inside keys. *Collection of J.Braithwaite*

Withington and West Didsbury, March 17th.1965: A melancholy picture taken from the end of the Up platform. Though the line has still a few years of life, the overall picture now is one of desolation. The tall, lattice-post Up home signal whose arms so often pointed skywards is out of use. Likewise, too, the little signalbox has been closed (on June 21st. 1964), its block bells and frame silent, with levers chained and pad-locked and its windows boarded over. Although the platforms remain, it is over three years now since they felt the stamp of feet or heard the slamming of carriage doors. Soon, only the demolition men will find a job to do here. Notice the obviously extended platform on the Down side of the line.   *E.M.Johnson*

Withington and West Didsbury, Summer 1958: Withington's second signalbox was built alongside the original structure. Though to the final Midland design, period 3, the replacement box actually opened in LMS days-on May 4th. 1924. Housing 10 levers in a Midland tappet frame, it survived the station's closure. Minor design changes are worth mentioning, apart from the different style of window frames; notice the later roof has no finials and that the nameboards are now carried under the eaves-a pure LMS innovation. A steel-posted upper-quadrant sema-phore has now replaced the charming little Mid-land "peg" with its white circle. *E.M.Johnson*

South of Withington c.1895: Taken from the bridge that carries Elm Road, West Didsbury, over the railway we view a Johnson 4-4-0 on the Up line with an express. The train, of decidedly mixed proportions, carries a Pullman carriage-almost certainly a Parlour Car-in the middle of the train. Leaving Withington Station behind, the railway is now in a deep cutting. The land to the right once housed allotments from which certain small boys, who ventured over the care-fully cultivated land to watch trains, were regu-larly chased away! A block of flats now covers this ground and the trackbed of the former rail-way has, sadly, all but disappeared under a wilderness of trees and shrubbery.
                    Collection of J.Braithwaite

Withington and West Didsbury Mid-1960s: The station buildings viewed from Lapwing Lane, the thoroughfare that passed alongside. The spacious, almost ecclesiastically-styled structure was almost identical with those at neighbouring Didsbury (q.v.) Towards the end of the decade, the buildings at Withington were demolished. A rather plain-looking block of flats known as "Lapwing Court" now covers the ground here. Only the rump of the wall on the right-hand side remains now as a testament to former glories.   *G.H.Platt*

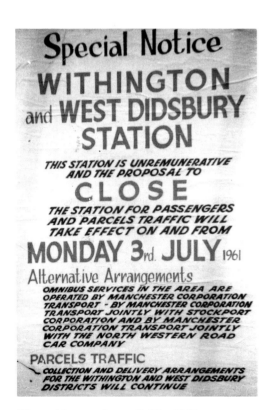

The writing on the wall: The 1960s were sorry times for the British Railway system. Beeching was pre-empted by several years with the withdrawal of South District line Local services and attendant station closures. Heaton Mersey station, also, closed at the same time.   *E.M.Johnson*

Withington and West Didsbury, December 4th. 1948: The end of Withington's southbound (Up) platform showing the splendid double-armed and bracketed semaphore which carried both Down home (facing the camera) and Up starter. Pity the poor lampman who would have had to climb the 80 or so rungs of the ladder week in, week out in all weathers to change the lamp! Just visible on the left of the picture are the remains of the original end screens to the platform canopies. These were installed some time after the S.D. line stations opened and were removed in modern times, along with two of the canopies, to reduce maintenance costs.   *R.E.Gee*

Withington and West Didsbury, Sunday July 2nd. 1961: Withington's last operational day seen on a dull, summer afternoon. Here we can see the platform side of the architecture previously glimpsed at road-level. Notice now the gaps in the brickwork; a drawing dated 1950 shows clearly the removal of the two bays of awning from the southern ends of the platforms. The original awnings had boarded fronts and glazed rear panels for roofing. These early B.R. economies caused the boarded fronts to be felted over, with corrugated asbestos cement sheeting taking the place of the middle glazed section. Only the rear part of the awning roof, as seen here, retained its glazing. These changes undoubtedly denied the station much of its character. Late in the evening on the day this picture was taken the Author had the dubious pleasure of being the last passenger to use the station here.   *E.M.Johnson*

West Didsbury, pre-WW1: As a brief interlude from the railway I thought it would be nice to step outside of what was then Withington and Albert Park station into what was effectively another world. Only the rattle of Manchester Corporation's electric tramcars and the clatter of horses' hooves disturb the quite idyllic scene at the junction of Palatine Road and Lapwing Lane. No motor cars harass the well-dressed pedestrians as they amble over the road. West Didsbury was very much a middle-class area in those days; this was the world of propriety, of the carte de visite, of the drawing room with its maid, and when Madam was mistress of all she surveyed. A world of gas lamps, of red and cream trams, and of straw Boaters. Forward over eighty years and the trams are back in Manchester. The ultimate irony will occur when they appear at West Didsbury again. This time they will glide under the road, taking the place of the railway that was king when this picture was taken.   *Collection of Raymond Keeley*

Withington and West Didsbury. c. 1961 : One of Trafford Park's 4Fs, No.**44565**, waits alongside the Up platform with a 3-coach Local. This view shows the station in decline: the end screens referred to earlier, have long gone, whilst the glazing in the platform canopies has been replaced by boarding and corrugated sheeting. *W.A.Brown*

Leaving Withington & West Didsbury, c.1956: "Jubilee" No.**45636** *Uganda* looks quite the picture-clean and smart with a rake of "blood and custard" carriages-as it heads south away from Withington with an express for St.Pancras. The landscape here has become unrecognisable since the line's closure in 1969, with wintertime often bringing smething of a small lake on this section of the trackbed. During Easter, 1991, the author photographed a family of Mallards swimming blithely along near the station. Peacefully waddling amidst the tall bullrushes and trees that have now seeded themselves, the little family showed how nature has regained its territory. Something of an impromptu widlife reserve perhaps, but a sad waste nevertheless. *N.F.W.Dyckhoff*

The Manchester South District - A Last Look

Those curious enough to want to see the last remains of this once-fine railway can make their way to the top of Burnage Lane, just off the A5145, in South Manchester. Down beyond the Green Pastures housing estate, where Heaton Mersey rubs shoulders with suburban Manchester, the enthusiast can thread his way along the "walkway" which centres along the trackbed of the former railway for a short distance. Alongside the Tesco store at East Didsbury runs the Styal line of the former LNWR; a few hundred yards beyond this, on the left-hand side, is the sea of silver-grey vehicles announcing the location of British Telecom's depot-sited on the former Didsbury goods yard. It was here that Archer, Haggis and Parker dutifully kept their train register and where, daily, Mr.Unsworth climbed the steps of the little box to make sure everything was in order.

Ahead now is the overbridge that takes a busy School Lane down to Wilmslow Road, notice the orangey tones of the brickwork for this is a new structure; like almost all the South District bridges it has been renewed at great expense in recent years pending the extension of the LRT system along here. Ignoring the green sign that points

him up to Didsbury, the intrepid traveller stumbles on through the undergrowth of blackberry thorns, weeds, trees and bushes and alights upon the remains of Didsbury Station, its platform faces and copings standing Ozymandias-like after over twenty years of disuse and recalling Shelley's immortal lines on the trunkless legs of stone in the desert: "Look on my works,ye Mighty, and despair."

Hardy souls can brave nature's wilderness and press on towards West Didsbury, taking care of the lake that sometimes forms here in the winter months. But, memories aside, there is little of railway interest to be seen in this wilderness. As this book goes to press, contractors are undertaking the difficult job of renewing the Palatine Road overbridge just beyond the site of West Didsbury station. This is the last bridge to be rebuilt, making the stretch of alignment between Old Trafford and East Didsbury into a viable form once again. If Metrolink is successful and spreads its wings to reclaim this valuable stretch of line, we will once more be able to travel over the route of the South District Railway.

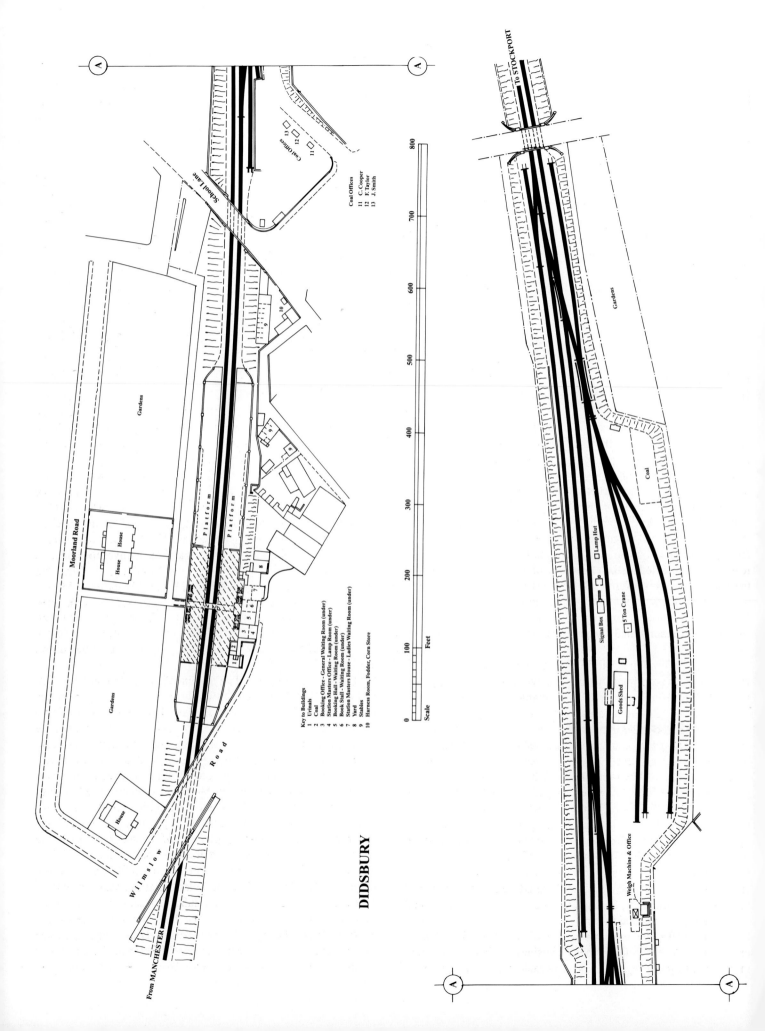

DIDSBURY

To STOCKPORT

From MANCHESTER

Moorland Road

Wilmslow Road

School Lane

Gardens

House

House

Platform

Platform

Coal Offices

Gardens

Coal

Goods Shed

Signal Box

Lamp Hut

5 Ton Crane

Weigh Machine & Office

Key to Buildings
1 Urinals
2 Coal
3 Booking Office - General Waiting Room (under)
4 Station Masters Office - Lamp Room (under)
5 Station Masters Office - Waiting Room (under)
6 Booking Hall - Waiting Room (under)
7 Book Stall - Waiting Room (under)
8 Station Masters House - Ladies Waiting Room (under)
9 Yard
10 Stables
11 Harness Room, Fodder, Corn Store

Coal Offices
11 C. Cooper
12 F. Taylor
13 J. Smith

Scale

0   100   200   300   400   500   600   700   800

Feet

Didsbury Station, December 21st.1952: The stately, distinguished lines of this once-familiar building seen barely four years after the inception of British Railways. Looking at the solid, Victorian architecture it seems incredible that all four South District stations were built for just over £15,000-a likely sum these days for a down payment on a terraced house in the village here! A period touch is provided by the motor car standing on the forecourt-where are you now KNE 851? Another item of interest stands out: the red telephone box by the station entrance, a rare sight now and something of a protected species.
A.C.Gilbert

Didsbury

Didsbury, the third of the South Manchester communities to be served by the Midland company's new line of 1880, was a thriving place even before the railway arrived, though its population did increase by 60% within the first decade or so of the railway's coming. The new station was in the heart of the village and was situated on the main Wilmslow Road, well placed to serve the local business and domestic market. Architecturally, the buildings at Didsbury were identical to those at neighbouring Withington, just under a mile down the line (actually 1272 yards). Unlike Withington though, Didsbury had the advantage of being sited well away from the omni-present tramcar and also possessed a goods yard of reasonable size. Sited on the Down side of the line and just south of the station itself, this offered full facilities, including a goods shed, milk dock and facilities for the transhipment of horses and livestock. Crane power, at up to 5 tons capacity, was also available. A lay-by siding with a capacity for 39 wagons was provided as well and stood on the Up side.

Right up to modern times Didsbury was thought important enough to warrant early morning (Up) and late evening (Down) expresses stopping there. The Summer 1954 timetable shows the 7.20 a.m., 9.00 and 10.00 (SO) expresses to St.Pancras calling to pick up passengers. All took 12 minutes from Central. In the Down direction the 4.15 p.m. from St.Pancras called at Didsbury at 8.34 to set down, likewise the 6.40 at 10.52. Forward ten years to Summer 1964 and we find the 7.25 a.m. Up train calling at 7.36 (taking one minute less please note!); the 8.25, likewise, stopped at 8.36. Returning from St.Pancras the Didsbury resident of twenty-eight years ago could choose between the 4.25 Down (stopping in the village station at 8.06) or the 6.55 p.m. calling at the still-respectable hour of 10.49-just too late for a pint in "The Railway" or "The Wellington" across the road! An interesting aside from a timetable study of those days is the use of musical "sharp" and "flat" signs to denote "pick up" and "set down" respectively. Perhaps today's "customers" are thought to be ignorant of musical theory!

Suburban traffic, the station's raison d'etre is worthy of brief examination. When the line opened for business, on January 1st.1880, most of the stopping trains (19 per day each way) ran on a through service from Manchester Central (old station) to London Road. This was accomplished by joint working between the Midland and the MS&L companies; the service ran via Didsbury, Stockport (Tiviot Dale) and Reddish (on the Sheffield & Midland Joint line from Romiley Junction) and from there into London Road.

Interestingly, this was not the first time that trains had run from Central to London Road. The MS&L had begun a circular service between the two stations on December 1st.1879. Using the MSJ&A line and a short curve from just beyond Timperely Station to Skelton Junction, the trains called at Baguley, Northenden and Cheadle (CLC) before running into Tiviot Dale and thence over the Joint line again back to London Road. One source has suggested that the service was put on at the behest of Sir Edward Watkin, the MS&L Chairman who lived at Rose Hill, a mansion just by Northenden Station; no official records have been found to prove this however. The MS&L service only lasted until March 1880 and the short-lived Timperley-Skelton curve fell out of use. Its track remained in situ until 1903 before lifting took place.

Manchester Central (new) station opened for traffic on July 1st.1880 and all local services were promptly transferred to it; main line traffic followed on August 2nd. M&SL involvement in South District local services lasted until the end of 1884; hereafter, the Midland were in sole charge. Few good archive photographs survive showing us what rolling stock these early Midland suburban services comprised. It is known that both four and six-wheeled stock was used; this would have been lit by gas, and some by oil. Things improved markedly in 1903 when David Bain's 48 ft., 8 ft. 6 ins. wide bogie arc-roofed suburban stock began to appear on the local services. Running in close-coupled sets of seven coaches each, and weighing 205 1/2 tons tare per set, the new stock comprised 28 first-class and 36 third-class compartments per rake of coaches. This set-up yielded 168 first and 360 third class seats per train-the highest first/third ratio of any Midland suburban service. It has been suggested that the influence of the high number of first-class contract (season) ticket holders may have had a bearing on this. The Bain arc-roofed sets were lit by gas and carried steam heating. They ran in their original form on the South District services until round

1928, when sources suggest that some of the first-class compartments were down-graded to third class status.

In 1910, a period which is regarded as the high-water mark for the British railway system, no less than 38 (Up) and 41 (Down) local trains called at Didsbury on regular weekday basis. This includes trains which ran only as far as Cheadle Heath as well as those that went beyond Chinley to Sheffield and Derby.

Perusal of modern timetables shows, of course, a marked reduction in the same services. The summer 1954 timetable shows 23 (Up) and 24 (Down) locals. Ten years later, 1954, and the service had gone downhill rapidly: just 13 (Up) and 12 (Down) locals called at Didsbury. By that time, both Withington and Heaton Mersey stations had closed and the service was in terminal decline.

Perusal of the LMSR rating plan for the 1920s shows the extent of railway ownership of the land in the vicinity of the station. Not only does this cover the station proper but extends to include what became shops just adjacent to the station, along with a number of buildings stretching as far as School Lane. Three of these buildings are shown as stables; also included are a harness room, a fodder store and the requisite manure bin! The whole of Moorland Road, leading from Wilmslow Road and connecting with the station via the footbridge, was also railway property. Ownership of this road must have extended into modern times as the road surface has never been properly "metalled"- the "company" probably deeming this an unnecessary piece of frippery! To this day Moorland Road retains its respectability with its "Private Road" sign. Signalling details at this time are at odds with those pertaining in later years.

Didsbury Station, Up Platform c.1964: Here we view the station from the southbound platform looking towards Manchester Central with just one passenger in sight. Alterations to the station from its early days included the removal in 1950 of two of the platform awnings (as at Withington) as evidenced by the blank gables in the brick walls on the left-hand side. The remaining glazing was replaced by corrugated sheeting and felted boarding. Notice the profusion of gas lamps and the now much-prized maroon LMR totems. Gas lighting remained a feature here until closure, even inside the buildings.   *G.H.Platt*

Didsbury Station, June 5th.1961: The Derbyshire spa town of Buxton once had the luxury of two separate rail services from Manchester. The Midland route, which, at 32¼ miles was just seven miles longer than that of the LNWR, followed a somewhat circuitous and steeply-graded path via Peak Forest. In the Beeching era, elimination of such duplication was de rigeur; trains to Buxton from Manchester Central were withdrawn on March 6th. 1967. On a lovely summer evening in early June, "Rebuilt Patriot" No. **45540** *Sir Robert Turnbull* heads through the glowing sunlight towards the Peak with the 5.22 p.m. express from Manchester Central to Buxton. Known as the "Buxton Club Train", the first stop was Cheadle Heath after which the train called at Chinley (where engine crews were changed-Buxton drivers taking over from the Trafford Park men), Chapel-en-le-Frith (Central) and Peak Forest. Arrival in Buxton was at 6.33.   *W.A.Brown*

Didsbury Station, winter 1951: For myself this picture says everything that I remember of trains on the South District line. A hazy winter atmosphere is broken by the thunderous exhaust of Class 5 No.**44938** as it tears through Didsbury with an Up express, thunders under School Lane and disappears up the line towards Heaton Mersey. Happy days, now long gone. *N.F.W.Dyckhoff*

Didsbury. 10th September 1954. This two-armed Midland-pattern semaphore with its sight boards was a distinctive feature of the station here for many years. Standing duty at the end of the Down platform it stood up against the bridge (No.12) which took Wilmslow Road (A34) over the South District line. Carrying the Down Starter for Didsbury and the Down Distant for Withington it lasted until April 1956 before being replaced by a colour light. As a footnote, bridge No.12 was all but life-expired when the line here closed in 1969. Dating from 1879, its nine cast-iron girders were giving cause for concern when single-lane traffic working was instituted on Wilmslow Road in the early 1960s. After closure the bridge was propped in the centre by means of a brick pier. Eventually, the stresses and strains of modern traffic were too much and a new bridge had to be constructed, although some of the lower brickwork on the jack arches was retained. Much the same remedy was adopted for other S.D. line bridges, all at great expense; awaiting the day when the LRT system arrives. *R.E.Gee*

Didsbury Station, The Last Days: One of the last photographs taken of a train calling at Didsbury Station. Two days prior to closure, on December 30th. 1966, locomotive No. **D5584** draws alongside the Up platform at the head of the 11.45 a.m. Manchester Central to Sheffield stopping train. Diesel power was certainly not a newcomer to the South District line and over the years a wide variety of types was recorded. Well-remembered were the two pioneers from 1947/48 Nos. 10000 and 10001, the Metrovick Co-Bos of 1958 numbered in the D5700 series and the curious Fell 2-D-2 Diesel-Mechanical locomotive-No. 10100. D5584, seen here, was one of a series of A1A-A1A configuration locomotives of 1,250 h.p. delivered by Brush Ltd. between 1957-62. Becoming Class 30 and 31, several examples are still at work on British Rail today. Didsbury Station closed after the passage of the 18.45 express from Central to St.Pancras on Sunday, January 1st.1967. Thus ended South District local services, exactly 87 years to the day after they began. *W.A.Brown*

Didsbury, School Lane bridge c.1951: With a thunderous exhaust, the safety valves lifting, and a bad steam leak, "Jubilee" No.45682 *Trafalgar* pulls away from Didsbury with an Up stopping train. For years it had been the intention to rebuild the School Lane overbridge and the girders for this purpose lay on the land behind the train throughout the 1950s. Nicknamed "The Didsbury Girders" by locals they were even re-painted regularly pending their installation . However, this ramshackle affair over the line was the nearest the authorities ever got to providing a new structure and the girders found use elsewhere. Finally, in 1986, a new bridge was completed-just seventeen years after the line closed!   *N.F.W.Dyckhoff*

Didsbury Signalbox, November 22nd. 1964: Tucked away in front of the goods yard, between School Lane and the back of Didsbury Park was Didsbury's Signalbox. As at Withington this was the second box on the same site. The original structure dated from the opening of the line, this one-to a Midland Period II design-opened on December 17th. 1899. Perusal of the train register for 1950 shows the box to be manned by Messrs. T.B.Archer, H.H.Haggis and A.Parker. Didsbury's Stationmaster in those days was Mr.J.W.Unsworth. The box closed on March 5th. 1967.   *M.A.King*

Didsbury Goods Yard, May 31st.1954: One of the ever-popular LMS Compounds, No. 41123, passes Didsbury's goods yard with the 1.04 Manchester Central to Sheffield stopping train. The premises backing onto the line belonged to Provincial Laundries Ltd; whisps of steam issuing from their boilers often giving false alarms to watching schoolboys further down the line!   *A.C.Gilbert*

Didsbury, bridge leading to School Lane winter 1954: An everyday sight at Didsbury in the 1950s was the arrival at 10.13 in the morning of the curious-looking Fell Diesel-Mechanical locomotive No.**10100**. Usually at the head of a stopping train from Derby, the Fell engine was something of a curiosity with its peculiar-looking red-painted outside coupling rods and bulbous "bonnets" at either end. Transmission apart, the Fell locomotive was unusual in that it used separate engines, one at each end; this was in contrast to later Diesel practice which, by and large, relied on the use of a single power unit. Here the 120 ton, 2,400 h.p. locomotive passes under the bridge from Didsbury Park to School Lane with an Up express. 10100 appears in the later condition in which the four coupled wheels had been split into two separate units. On October 15th. 1958 the Fell engine caught fire at Manchester Central. Following this, it was taken to Derby Works where it was cut up in 1960.   *N.F.W.Dyckhoff*

Didsbury. n.d. Over the Fields and Far Away: Taken from the footpath which today connects Sandhurst Road with School Lane, this is a view of the railway c.1922 looking up the line towards Heaton Mersey. The land to the left of the track was situated between Whitehall Farm and School Lane Farm; the fence alongside the field bounded a footpath which crossed the railway via an occupation bridge-just visible in the distance. The footpath was a continuation of School Lane and terminated in a junction with Wilmslow Road-across from East Didsbury and Parr's Wood Station on the LNWR's Styal line. The little Midland "peg" was Didsbury's Up Starter; a hardy specimen, it lasted until 1958 before being supplanted by a colour light further down the line in front of the present day Parr's Wood Road overbridge.   *Railway Revivals collection*

Occupation Bridge leading to Parr's Wood c.1922: This is the occupation bridge mentioned in the previous picture. Known as "Webb's Bridge" and numbered 8 in the Midland Railway Ambergate District bridge register, it lasted until the present-day Parr's Wood Road was built in 1926. This spanned the railway at right-angles and was sited some 30 or so yards nearer to Didsbury's goods yard. At the same time the splendid splitting Distant signal for Heaton Mersey Station Junction was removed and replaced further up the line. (q.v.)   *Railway Revivals collection*

Site of Webb's Bridge, May 12th. 1948: From the same spot as the picture of the Class 3 we look at a changed landscape 26 years on in time with LMS No. **88**, one of Stanier's Class 3 2-6-2 tank locomotives, heading a 5-coach Up stopping train. Semi-detached houses have mushroomed up along the line and the fields of Whitehall Farm have given way to the back gardens of Kingsfield Drive. These days, only the traffic passing along the present day Parr's Wood Road now disturbs this corner of suburbia.
R.E.Gee

Webb's Bridge, looking towards Didsbury c.1922: With Whitehall Farm in the background we move back in time to pre-Grouping days to glimpse Class 3 "Belpaire" 4-4-0 No. **759** heading towards Heaton Mersey with an Up express. Just visible is the splitting Distant for Heaton Mersey Station Junction; the lower arm is pegged "off" indicating that our train is taking the "old" route via Heaton Mersey East Junction, Stockport Tiviot Dale and Marple.
Railway Revivals collection

Styal Line overbridge March 28th. 1959: Taken from the Kingsway bridge the now electrified Styal Line (Slade Lane Junction to Wilmslow) forms a background to this splendid shot of "Black 5" No.**44665** gathering speed between Didsbury and Heaton Mersey with a Manchester Central to Derby stopping train. *Tom Lewis*

Heaton Mersey Station Junction, Up Distant Signals, August 12th. 1954: These splendid Midland Railway-pattern semaphore signals, with their pressed steel corrugated arms, were replacements for the ones seen earlier which stood in front of Webb's Bridge. Now standing between the Styal Line and the A34 thoroughfare known as Kingsway, bridging the line in the background, the signals exemplify early LMS practice whereby existing designs of the dominant constituent company were used as something of a stop-gap. The arms repeat the diverging routes mentioned earlier and the "pegs" survived until May 1958 when their replacement, a 3-aspect colour light, appeared-back more or less in the original position! Notice the superb condition of the recently relaid permanent way-the old bullhead chairs and sleepers lying abandoned at the side of the line. *R.E.Gee*

Styal Line overbridge June 6th.1948: One of the all-time classic pictures of trains on the South District line is, surely, this view of No.**34005** *Barnstaple* storming up the 1-in-160 gradient to Heaton Mersey with the 1.50 Manchester Central to St.Pancras express during the interchange trials of 1948. The sight of a locomotive from such far-off "foreign" parts must have been a wonderful occasion, especially when the visitor was so well turned out as this. The Stanier tender was a necessary appendage for London Midland running, Southern engines lacking the necessary water pick-up apparatus.   *R.E.Gee*

Looking to Burnage Lane/Didsbury Road overbridge May 23rd.1954: Taken from the Kingsway road bridge, this Summer view sees "Jubilee" No. **45655** *Keith* speeding down the line from Heaton Mersey with an express bound for Manchester Central. The alignment of the South District Railway today finishes just about where the rear coach of the express is. Here the present-day "walkway" commences down to School Lane amidst a landscape changed out of all recognition from those halcyon days.   *B.K.B.Green*

Looking towards Heaton Mersey, June 1951: Giving overtones of former ownership, "Jubilee" No.**45696** *Arethusa* pulls away from Heaton Mersey station and heads down the line towards Didsbury with a stopping passenger train. It is from here, where the ground is covered with fresh summer grass and wild flowers, that the alignment of the railway has today been lost: the Green Pastures housing estate now occupies the land to the right of where the photographer is stood. Across in the left foreground are the backs of the terraced houses along Chapel Street. Today, the houses remain, neat and well-kept; behind, along the top of the remains of the shallow cutting, can be seen the iron railings which once formed the boundary between railway and alley-way-just about the only tangible reminder of scenes such as this. *N.F.W.Dyckhoff*

After leaving Didsbury and passing under the junction of Parr's Wood Lane and Didsbury Road, the line entered the boundaries of Stockport. Here, Cheshire was encountered and the railway fell upon the district of Heaton Mersey, one of the four "Heatons" that are so confusing to those who do not know this little corner of the world. Between Didsbury and Heaton Mersey the line was on a rising gradient varying between 1-in-150 and 1-in-400 up to Heaton Mersey Station Junction where the line bifurcated. Here the original South District railway had dropped down from its junction with the Cheshire Lines system at Heaton Mersey East. In 1902 Heaton Mersey Station Junction was created when the New Mills and Heaton Mersey Line was opened via Disley Tunnel and Cheadle Heath from New Mils South Junction.

Goods facilities were provided at Heaton Mersey from the time of the station's opening. These were enlarged in later years, in particular an extended headshunt, two cart roads and coal drops were provided, the latter were sited between the station and Vale Road for Melland and Coward's bleach works, part of which still stands today on the north bank of the River Mersey.

Station and Junction apart, Heaton Mersey also possessed an important engine shed. This was sited off the Cheshire Lines system at Heaton Mersey West Junction and was situated south of the running lines above the banks of the Mersey overlooking the district of Gorsey Bank. Above the shed and hard by the through lines were Heaton Mersey Sidings, a complex extending east towards Stockport.

Heaton Mersey Station, n.d: Viewed from the path down from Grundy Hill Farm that crossed the railway via bridge No. this was the last of the South District's stations; like the others, it dated from the opening of the line in January, 1880. Notice the depth of the cutting here, a massive landfill operation was needed after the line was closed-obliterating almost every last vestige of the railway. *W.J.Skillern*

Heaton Mersey Station n.d: These fine buildings standing on the Up platform were unlike any others on the line and bore more than a passing resemblance to those on the CLC system over the fields at Cheadle. Dipping down to cross the line is the unusual lattice footbridge which connected the station with Didsbury Road. The short gas lamps mounted on top of the brick wall pillars were a feature seen at other S.D. line stations. Stephens' Ink, Beecham's Powders and Earles Cement are all popular wares advertised here via the now valuable enamelled signs.   *Author's collection*

Heaton Mersey Station. c.1951. B.R.Standard Mogul No. **76089** runs in with a semi-fast train from Manchester Central, probably bound for Sheffield. Heaton Mersey's out of the way location, coupled with its steeply-graded access road made it an unpopular choice with passengers. Even in pre-Group days passenger bookings here were half, or even less, than those at neighbouring Didsbury. Even so, in a modern context, there is ample evidence that stations like Heaton Mersey have enjoyed a new lease of life when their redundant goods yards have been turned into car parks and passengers have been encouraged to use the trains.   *W.A.Brown*

Heaton Mersey Station, April 25th. 1922: At the head of an Up stopping train is rebuilt Johnson Class 2 4-4-0 No. **447**. Notice, again, the unusual split-level footbridge complete with short-pattern gas lamp.   *Author's collection*

Heaton Mersey Station Junction, September 18th. 1964: A splendid summer scene looking south across the junction as "Type 4" Diesel No.**D87** speeds past with the 8.05 a.m. St.Pancras-Manchester Central express. The original route to Stockport can just be made out curving away in the left background. Notice the various semaphores: three carry slotted distant arms for (left to right) Heaton Mersey East, Cheadle Heath North and (on the Down line) for Didsbury. At first glance all looks well in the world; but pause for a moment. Alongside the Up line see how the connection to the goods yard has now been severed. (It was offically closed on October 7th.1963). The train, too, is indicative of the line's ultimate fortunes for this is one of the lengthened formations-up to 11 coaches-introduced in 1962 to take the pressure off the London Road-Euston services pending electrification. Once that was complete, in 1966, the Midland line was doomed. As at Withington and Didsbury, the signal box here was a replacement for a previous structure: this box dated from September 22nd. 1901. In anticipation of the opening of the "New" line through Cheadle Heath to New Mills the following year, it was re-named "Heaton Mersey Station Junction" just one week later. Closure came on March 5th. 1967, just over two months after the section of line from here to Heaton Mersey East had been abandoned.

Heaton Mersey Station Junction, July 26th. 1952: With a 7-coach stopping train LMS Compound No. **41056** runs down off the "Old" line-the original South District route from Heaton Mersey East Junction on the CLC-towards Heaton Mersey station. The line through Cheadle Heath and Disley tunnel curves away to the right; the slotted Distant signal is for Cheadle Heath North Junction. When the "new" line was opened, in 1902, the Stockport route was re-aligned with a very sharp curve necessitating a 15 m.p.h. speed restriction. A bad derailment occured in the early 1930s when Class 3 4-4-0 No. 330 came to grief with a Down train just short of the junction. Following this the junction was re-modelled and the curve to the Stockport line eased. The fields to the left of the railway are typical of the open nature of the landscape round here and form a curious buffer between suburban South Manchester and a heavily built-up Stockport. *B.K.B.Green*

Heaton Mersey station, 1947: Johnson 2F 0-6-0 No.**22929** performs the daily shunt at Heaton Mersey station yard. Here the main line is behind us and we are looking across the goods yard towards Didsbury Road. In the background is Melland and Coward's upper bleach works; the neat terrace of houses in front were situated along what was Park Row and Park Place. All this is now history with Craig Road and the adjacent light industrial estate filling the foreground where once the clanking of buffers echoed.   *N.R.Knight*

Heaton Mersey, view above Station Junction August 23rd. 1958: In this pleasing panorama we look down onto the surroundings of Heaton Mersey, its trees and fields rubbing shoulders with the conurbation of South Stockport. In the foreground a four-coach train runs along the South District, away from Heaton Mersey Station Junction and on up to Stockport Tiviot Dale. Curving away in the foreground is the "new" line crossing the Mersey towards Cheadle Heath. Here, at Cheadle Heath North Junction the "Liverpool Curve" can be made out above the far bank of the river. Forming the base of a triangle, the CLC main line crosses the river and dives under the high-level bridge past Heaton Mersey shed and on towards Heaton Mersey East Junction. Readily discernible, too, is Heaton Mersey West box, the twin gables of the coaling stage and the westerly end of Heaton Mersey sidings.   *Raymond Keeley*

Heaton Mersey, High-Level bridge, Summer 1973: Taken after the line had closed, this view shows the bridge that carried the "new" line of 1902 from Heaton Mersey Station Junction along to Cheadle Heath, then via Disley Tunnel to New Mills South Junction. Above the left bank of the tranquil-looking River Mersey can be seen the semaphores controlling the spur line, the "Liverpool Curve" of 1902, from Cheadle Heath North Junction round to the CLC Glazebrook to Godley line at Cheadle Junction. The CLC line itself crosses the river just beyond the high-level structure. Behind this line can be seen the tall chimney of the Melland and Coward bleach works for which the Midland provided coal drops at Heaton Mersey goods yard. The high-level bridge was demolished in 1974, that taking the CLC line over the Mersey met a similar fate in 1986. Nowadays the air here rings incessantly with the noise of traffic speeding along the adjacent M63 Motorway. Now, only the the rippling current of the river and the occasional freight train threading its way along the single line to and from Northenden on the former CLC interrupts the roar of "progress." *Raymond Keeley*

Between Heaton Mersey and Cheadle Heath, August 1959: "Jubilee" No. **45620** *North Borneo* clears Heaton Mersey Station Junction and begins to dip down the 1-in-132 towards Cheadle Heath North Junction. The high-level bridge over the CLC line and the River Mersey are just behind the photographer. Beginning at 1-in-200 through Cheadle Heath, the line will start to climb remorselessly all the way to Peak Forest. Though the train carries express lights, six of the seven coaches are comprised of ex-Midland Railway Bain arc-roofed Suburban stock. Things Midland really were built to last! *Don Capper*

Heaton Mersey, High-Level Bridge, August 14th. 1952: An outstanding shot of "Jubilee" No. **45585** *Hyderabad* as it storms along, high above the River Mersey, at the head of a Manchester Central to St.Pancras express and dashes towards Cheadle Heath. Anyone who has tried to photograph moving trains, particularly at high speeds such as this and at such a sharp angle, will be aware of the acute difficulty that such a task presents. A remarkable shot from a photographer who was a master of his craft. *Tom Lewis*

Heaton Mersey, shed yard and CLC line, August 1959: Taken from the high-level bridge that carried the "new" line over the Mersey and into Cheadle Heath, we look towards Stockport town centre with focal points marked out by mill chimneys and high-rise flats. This most interesting view shows 4F No. **44080** ambling along past Heaton Mersey West Junction with a Stockport Tiviot Dale to Warrington stopping train. Running in at a tangent on the far left-hand side is the original alignment of the South District Railway-from Heaton Mersey East to Heaton Mersey Station Junction. East Junction signalbox can just be identified, to the immediate left of the home and distant semaphores behind the train. Running across the picture (from left to right) are no less than seven running lines giving an indication of the very busy nature of this stretch of line at that time. The tracks are: Up Goods Loop, Up Main, Down Main (on which the train is running), Up Fast Goods, Up Slow Goods (here are Heaton Mersey Sidings), Down Fast Goods, Down Slow Goods. The line curving away on the far right-hand side is the entry to Heaton Mersey Shed. *Don Capper*

Heaton Mersey West Junction, August 23rd. 1958: Just one year before the previous shot was taken, Raymond Keeley took this "opposite hand" view showing Heaton Mersey West Junction signalbox with its environment of loco shed and sidings clearly visible. Across to the right can be seen the rows of terraced houses on Gorsey Bank-home to many of the men who spent an entire lifetime in this vicinity. The high-level bridge casts a strong shadow over the track, allowing our old friend No. **40001** a chance to pose briefly in the summer sunshine. Heaton Mersey shed closed for good on May 6th. 1968. Incredibly, from this same viewpoint today, only a barren landscape is visible. The M63 motorway was built hard alongside the alignment of the trackbed of the CLC line, covering the ground where Heaton Mersey shed once stood. With shed, sidings and both main line bridges gone, only ghosts and pictures such as this are left now to evoke the memory of Heaton Mersey. *Raymond Keeley*

Heaton Mersey engine shed was sited on the south side of the CLC's Glazebrook to Godley line. Tucked away hard above the river bank, the shed overlooked Gorsey Bank and Brinksway Bank where once cotton mills and a leather works had been situated. Here, rows of terraced dwellings housed a populace, typical northern working folk and the backbone of the local industry of which the railway was once so much inextricably a part. Between the shed and the main line were the Heaton Mersey Sidings, once part of a complex weave of goods yards that stretched just beyond the LNWR's famous viaduct which spanned the CLC line before the latter thrust itself deep into the sandstone bowels of the town en route for Tiviot Dale.

Shared between the Midland and the Great Central, the depot had opened for traffic in January, 1889. Of the shed's eight roads the Midland Railway occupied the most southerly four. Beginning life as Midland shed No. 21B under the auspices of Belle Vue, it was known to us teenage enthusiasts of the late 1950s as 9F. Previously coded 17E-as part of the Derby district (no less)-Heaton Mersey had received a variety of codes over the years, having been controlled by a number of different authorities including Longsight.

Heaton Mersey Shed, c.early 1890s: One of S.W.Johnson's magnificent series of Singles, No. **1865**, stands on the 50'-0" turntable at Heaton Mersey shed. These incredibly elegant-looking machines had a charm, beauty and grace that was, surely, unique in the whole genre of Victorian locomotive engineering. Built at Derby in December 1889, No. 1865 was one of a batch of five Singles, or "Spinners" as they were known, which ran with 7'-6" drivers. The sharp-eyed may have detected the lack of "MR" initials on the tender, a practice not adopted until 1892.

Railway Revivals collection

Heaton Mersey Shed, coaling stage 1930s: One of the least attractive aspects of the steam locomotive was its sheer dependency on human toil for maintenance. Though this view takes us back in time some sixty years or so, the coaling stage here, with its primitive facilities, was still extant in modern times. Loaded coal wagons were propelled up the ramp to the back of the stage whereupon their contents were shovelled into the small tubs seen being handled by the two men. The tubs were then tipped forward, the contents spilling into the waiting tenders. No. **5853** was one of Harry Pollitt's 11A 4-4-0s built between 1897/99 for service on the Great Central's newly-opened London Extension. Becoming LNER class D6, they spent their declining years on secondary passenger services. This included work on Manchester to Liverpool expresses over the CLC. Whilst at Heaton Mersey, in company with two other D6s, No. 5853 would have worked stopping trains to and from Liverpool Central to Godley via Warrington, Glazebrook and Stockport Tiviot Dale. 5853 was withdrawn in April, 1946. *W.Potter*

Heaton Mersey, shed yard, September 17th. 1965: "Jubilee" No. **45705** *Seahorse* achieved something of celebrity status from September 1964 when it became a regular performer on the Manchester Central to Buxton expresses. "Seahorse" was usually in charge of the 8.00 a.m. Down train and the 5.22 p.m. Up service. Like many express locomotives in the latter days of steam, Seahorse lost its nameplates, actually in March 1965. Credit must be given to the members of the Buxton Model Engineering Society who provided and fixed replicas in the August of that year. Here, No. 45705 is about to take charge of an LCGB excursion train from Cheadle Heath to Birmingham. "Seahorse" worked at its post on the Buxton trains until the very end of its life. It was withdrawn on November 10th. 1965.

W.A.Brown

Heaton Mersey Shed, Coaling Stage, 1950s: A rare peep inside the coaling stage showing the locomotive coal being shovelled out of the 16-ton wagons into the small skips; these two chaps certainly earned their bread and butter! These are then unloaded into the loco tenders as described. Waiting skips can be seen in the right-hand side of the picture. *P.Ward*

Heaton Mersey Shed. Summer 1966. Two turntables appear to have existed at Heaton Mersey; this one, on the shed's north side - close by the CLC main line - was re-instated on a previously disused site. The table itself, a 70 foot specimen, was removed from the MSJ&A side of Manchester's London Road in 1958 following the re-modelling of that side of the station ready for the electrification programme to Crewe. It is believed that this turntable was installed to replace the previous one, which stood in front of the main running shed, when this became unusable. 8F 2-8-0 No.**48503** looks ready for special duty with the number "8X57" chalked on the smokebox. In these, the closing years of the shed's life, evidence of dereliction looms large: notice the overgrown sidings in the background and the rising presence of the Diesel depot; something, alas, that never materialised here. *Mike Osborne.*

East of Heaton Mersey the Midland were on joint territory-that belonging to the CLC whose main line they traversed from Heaton Mersey East Junction through Stockport Tiviot Dale as far as Bredbury Junction. Here was the 1 mile, 24 chain branch from Romiley where the Great Central and Midland Joint line, the Midland's original springboard into the City of Manchester, had turned off towards Woodley and Hyde to the original terminus of Manchester London Road.

(Above) **Heaton Mersey Sidings, east end n.d**: Viewed from Didsbury Road, this is the east end of Heaton Mersey sidings, somewhat occluded by a smokescreen from a passing 8F. Stretching for just over half a mile, this complex stretched almost as far as Heaton Mersey West from where we viewed the 4F with the Stockport to Warrington train.
A.K.Rathbone

Georges Road Junction signalbox n.d: This impressive CLC-pattern brick-built signalbox with its 53-lever frame controlled the operations at Georges Road. The term "junction" was something of a misnomer when used in the strict sense; the track layout here simply splitting in the Down direction to form parallel goods lines between this point and Heaton Mersey West Junction. An extra pair of lines-Down Fast and Down Slow Goods-ran between Heaton Mersey Sidings signalbox and Heaton Mersey West.
Raymond Keeley

Georges Road Junction January 26th.1967: 8F No.**48161** pulls a Down freight up and away from the tunnel under Wellington Road. To the right of the picture can be seen the abandoned trackwork of the Wellington Road goods yard.
Gordon Coltas

Georges Road

Passing under Didsbury Road just outside Stockport town centre, the CLC line paralleled Travis Brow before coming upon the mass of sidings at Georges Road. Here, the cluster of lines could be divided into roughly four parts: i) The Club House sidings and the siding serving the adjacent timber yard; these were situated on the north side of the line and lay immediately in front of the Didsbury Road bridge. ii) Georges Road sidings proper; fourteen sidings which were fanned out on the north side of the through lines along the thoroughfare of Georges Road. iii) Georges Road

Junction; the point where the goods lines, which we saw terminating at Heaton Mersey West, split from the Up and Down lines running westwards from Tiviot Dale station. iv) The Wellington Road goods depot. This was sited on the south side of the line immediately under the east side of the LNWR's spectacular viaduct carrying the Manchester-Crewe line high above the town. Wellington Road goods was reached off Railway Street, itself just off the main A6 Wellington Road North above Mersey Square.

Georges Road n.d: A splendid view showing the whole of the Georges Road junction and siding complex. The photographer has his back to the LNW viaduct with the view towards Heaton Mersey straight ahead. With steam shut off an 8F runs along the Up main line with a train of petrol tankers and descends towards the gloom of the three tunnels thrust through the sandstone between here and Tiviot Dale. Behind the wall alongside the train can be seen the disused, grass-grown sidings of Wellington Road Goods. Georges Road sidings, sprouting still-plentiful signs of traffic, stand in the foreground and spread out to the right. The signal box can be seen to the right of the wagons, roughly in the middle of the train. Behind the box, the curiously-named Clubhouse sidings can be discerned. The highway of Georges Road itself was crossed by the railway via an impressive steel girder bridge. This can be made out by the presence of the overhead lattice bracing which was arched over the goods lines, to the left of the train. All around this once-everyday scene is the township of Heaton Norris, another of the "Heatons" in urban Stockport. On the left of the railway is Norris Street, behind this, Heaton Lane. Beyond, the cotton mills with their vast chimneys reaching skywards- Sheep Wash Mill, India Mills, Travis Brook Mill, all leading down to Brinksway Road and, out of sight, the murky, foaming waters of the River Mersey. Today, the vast empire of B & Q stands astride the scene where the trains and wagons of Georges Road were once assembled. One pillar of the Georges Road bridge remains - a monument if you like to the transport system that ruled here for so long. To the left of the picture the M63 Motorway has long since swept all before it: gone for ever the houses, mills, streets and people.　　　　*A.K.Rathbone*

Between Georges Road and Tiviot Dale n.d: Clear of Georges Road and the Wellington Road tunnel, trains heading towards Stockport Tiviot Dale passed through this cleft in the sandstone alongside Stewart Street, then under Hatton Street, from where this picture was taken, before penetrating the gloom of two further tunnels and passing under Lancashire Hill to arrive in Tiviot Dale itself. The signals were outer homes for the station platforms and survived until closure. Standing astride the horizon is the mighty LNWR's viaducts carrying the Manchester-Crewe line into Edgeley Station. The M63 motorway now runs along the left-hand side of the picture, hard by the alignment of the railway. Though not taken over by the motorway, as was once envisaged, the former trackbed has, within the last year, been partially covered with spoil, all but obliterating the scene here.

A.K.Rathbone

Stockport Tiviot Dale Station n.d: After burrowing deep through three sandstone tunnels-Wellington Road, Brownsord and Tiviot Dale-trains arrived at Stockport's Tiviot Dale station. Opened in 1865 the station was notable for two things: firstly, its superb architecture-thirty bays of fine brickwork set around the main building: an impressive Dutch-gabled centrepiece. And, secondly, its prime location in the heart of the town, close to the main business and shopping centre. Little traffic was in evidence when this picture was taken, just one Ford Anglia, a Zephyr and a Hillman Minx. "Park and ride" was a phrase yet to enter the public consciousness at that time. Tiviot Dale was now at the bottom of a long slope of decline. This culminated in closure in January 1967; worse followed-the magnificent structure was completely demolished in the summer of 1968.   *G.K.Fox collection*

Stockport Tiviot Dale, December 29th. 1966: Looking at the remains of the line today, it hardly seems possible that this stretch of railway was once one of the country's busiest freight lines, with trains literally "queuing up" to fit into the bottleneck between Cheadle Exchange Sidings and Skelton Junction. Exemplifying this torrent of traffic, 8F No.48119 breezes through Tiviot Dale with an Up wagon empties heading towards Portwood and Brinnington Junction. The curved footbridge was a characteristic of the station, along with the smoke that forever used to hang around the mouth of the tunnel from which the train has just emerged.

Gordon Coltas

Stockport Tiviot Dale, 1966: With "Crosti" 9F No. **92022** busying itself on the Down through road, we look west towards the Alligator Mill gleaning in the process some idea of the through nature of the station. Between the mouth of the Tiviot Dale tunnel and the signalbox seen in the distance were four tracks. The middle pair were the through lines and were used principally by freight trains-traffic which made up the vast bulk of the line's throughput. Two main platforms were provided at Tiviot Dale; the outer faces of each providing extra accommodation for local and excursion work. *A.K.Rathbone*

Tiviot Dale n.d: Derby-based 4F No.**44428** passes along the through road past Tiviot Dale's signalbox. An all-timber structure, this was once one of two boxes here-the one in our picture bearing the title "Tiviot Dale East." *H.Challoner*

Tiviot Dale, May 1961: With the luxury of at least five coaches, some of which consisted of first-class accommodation, the 11.40 all-stations Manchester Central to Chinley gets under way, with "Jubilee" No.**45607** *Fiji* at its head. Past the Alligator mill the train heads towards Portwood, Brinnington and Bredbury watched by two young spotters. Strange how anachronistic-looking Duffle coats, school caps and long grey socks have become!   *H.Challoner*

Tiviot Dale, late 1890s: The superb outlines of a Johnson 4-4-0, No.**1332** of Class G, seen as it pulls away east from the station. Built by Dubs, of Glasgow, in 1877 these very handsome machines with 7'-0" coupled wheels would have been daily performers on the Manchester-St.Pancras expresses, not forgetting the through portions to Liverpool. At the time this picture was taken all through Midland traffic travelled via Stockport and Marple making for much congestion. It was this that caused the Midland to look for an alternative route-the cut-off line of 1902 via Disley and Cheadle Heath being the result. Notice, in particular, the "East" suffix to the signal box name.   *J.Braithwaite collection*

Portwood Arches, March 30th.1962: East of Tiviot Dale the railway was carried through the district of Portwood via a series of bridges-no less than eighteen were needed to link Tiviot Dale with Brinnington. Portwood had been the site of the first station (before Tiviot Dale opened) in the vicinity, lasting until September 1875. In this view, that depicts something of the rather ramshackle nature of the area at that time, O4/8 No.**63895** rumbles over John Street with the 1.55 p.m.Northwich to Mansfield freight.   *Gordon Coltas*

Through Stockport Tiviot Dale and Portwood the CLC line ran north-eastwards towards Brinnington Junction. From this point a short spur ran due north to join the Romiley to Ashburys line, of 1875, at Reddish Junction. Running on towards the suburb of Bredbury, another junction was encountered; this was Bredbury Junction where different territory-this time Great Central & Midland Joint-was passed over. Paralleling the Romiley to Ashburys line, though at a lower level, this so-called "Marple curve" or "low-level" line, 1 mile, 24 chains long, ran through a cutting, a short tunnel and over the Peak Forest Canal to approach Romiley alongside both of the Midland's previous routes to Manchester: the original route from New Mills via Hyde and Guide Bridge over which passenger traffic had first passed in 1867 and the later Romiley to Ashburys line via Reddish and Belle Vue of 1875. It was the Bredbury low-level line that had given the Midland yet another route to Manchester-via Stockport and the Manchester South District Railway.

Brinnington Junction, November 1955: A rather grey, wintery view, looking east, of Brinnington Junction box-a CLC all-timber structure with a 40-lever frame. The CLC line runs straight ahead towards Brinnington Tunnel, the Great Central & Midland Joint line, 1 mile, 22 chains, runs off to the left to join the Ashburys line at Reddish Junction south-east of Reddish Vale viaduct. Known locally as the Portwood Branch, the line to Reddish Junction closed in September 1965; the junction was taken out of use in 1966.   *Dr. I. Scrimgeour, courtesy of the Signalling Record Society.*

Brinnington Tunnel, east end April 15th.1967: Trains leaving Stockport faced an uphill slog: 1-in-82 through Brinnington, steepening to 1-in-63 past Bredbury Junction. With what looks like an all-out effort, 9F 2-10-0 No.**92157** bursts out of the eastern portal of Brinnington tunnel and heads towards suburban Bredbury.   *A.K.Rathbone*

East of Brinnington Tunnel, September 11th.1966: 8F No.**48631** clears Brinnington Tunnel at seven minutes past four with the rear of its train still inside the bore. Nowadays, the alignment of the railway is lost beyond here. As Keith Rathbone so very ably took this splendid series of pictures I'll let him fill in the details in his own words: "This photograph was taken from the top of the "Camel's Hump", a geological peculiarity composed of moraine sand. I often wondered why there should be so much sand inland near Bredbury. This was a most pleasant location from which to observe trains working uphill towards Woodley, and the afternoon sun caught the trains well, as here, but it was a long way to run for cover if it rained!"
A.K.Rathbone

Brinnington Tunnel, east end June 10th.1966: Eleven minutes past three in the afternoon sees another 9F. This time No.**92162** drifts cautiously downhill into the tunnel with a loose-coupled freight, the 30 m.p.h. speed restriction looming up at the other end no doubt being on the driver's mind. Since the railway here was abandoned this stretch of line has been made into something of a feature: the tunnel lining has been whitewashed and a short piece of pre-fabricated track, together with a potted history of the line, has been put on display. Known now as part of the "Tiviot Country Park" it is possible to walk as far as Reddish Junction in the north and up to just about where the line curves away eastwards. Beyond that point no progress is possible; the M63 motorway now cuts a vast, sweeping curve, chasm-like, and altering irretrievably the landscape here. With the entire eastern suburbs of Stockport deprived of rail access to the town, one can only view with incredulity that such folly was ever perpetuated. *A.K.Rathbone*

Between Brinnington and Bredbury, September 11th.1966: Standing again on the "Camel's Hump" Keith has turned around to face Bredbury. Class 5 No.**44888** with a stopping passenger train comes face to face with 9F No.**92107** at the head of a Down freight consisting mostly of open wagons. In this scene, a curious mixture of open country and suburbia, the passenger train is passing the splitting distants for Bredbury Junction. The higher arm controls the short section of CLC line between there and Woodley; the lower one the "Marple curve" or low-level line round to Romiley Junction. *A.K.Rathbone*

At Bredbury Junction the line lay in shallow cutting. Here a small brick-built signalbox with an 18-lever frame controlled the short length of line round to Romiley Junction and the section along to Woodley Junction from where lines to Godley in the east and Hyde in the north could be accessed.

Bredbury Junction. n.d. An "Austin Seven" or Hughes/Fowler 0-8-0 No.**49624** clears the junction with a Down coal train consisting of around 24 wagons. Coal trains comprised much of the traffic over this route and lasted until modern times when an accident to the rock superstructure over the tunnel lining between Tiviot Dale and Georges Road sealed the line's fate. The lattice-post semaphores were something of a speciality at CLC locations, although other companies, notably the LMS and LNER also used the genre.   *W.A. Brown.*

Bredbury Junction. September 24th 1959. 8F No.**48695** crosses over the junction at Bredbury and takes the Woodley line with a trainload of standard 16-ton mineral wagons. In the bottom of the picture the "Bredbury Curve" (sometimes "Romiley Curve") runs off to Romiley. This short, but very useful section of line, closed to traffic from March 5th. 1967. Pending re-instatement, it was left in situ before being lifted in the summer of 1975. Thus was the centre of Stockport cut off completely from its eastern suburbs.   *W.A. Brown.*

Bredbury Junction. n.d. The low-level line running round to Romiley Junction is clearly seen here as O4/3 2-8-0 No.**63641** leads its train of mixed freight under the viaduct carrying the Romiley to Ashburys line away from Romiley and on towards Hyde and Guide Bridge. Behind the tender are two ICI tank wagons carrying bulk caustic soda. This traffic survives today in trainload form and can be seen travelling via Cheadle Heath, the Liverpool Curve and Northenden Junction - sad remnants of a once-busy network.   *W.A. Brown.*

Bredbury Tunnel "bottom" line. c.1953. LMS Compound 4-4-0 No.**41062** runs out of Bredbury Tunnel and along the low-level line towards Romiley Junction with an Up stopping train. By the lineside fence, just below the houses in Georges Lane, two small boys are watching the train. One of them, a very young Mr Gregory Fox, could have had little idea that he would appear some day in one of his own books!   *The late Cyril Fox.*

Bredbury, low-level line May 3rd. 1952: The Up low-level line Distant is ''on'' so 8F 2-8-0 No.**48323** from (8D) ambles slowly along towards Romiley Junction with its trainload of wooden- bodied wagons. A nice vintage touch is provided by the ganger walking along in the ''four foot.'' Long before the days of the mandatory high-visibility orange vest, our friend wears a short- sleeved pullover in the famous ''cable'' stitch, a tie (yes!) and Trilby hat.   *B.K.B.Green*

Bredbury, low-level line. April 13th 1952. With the boiler being topped up with the exhaust steam injector, Class 5 No.**44664** comes round the curve under the Quarry Road bridge before running along the straight section that parallelled the Ashburys line (seen on the right) to Romiley.   *B.K.B. Green.*

Approach to Romiley Junction, March 3rd.1952: From the bridge that led to Quarry Road we look towards the line via Hyde and Woodley-the Midland's first route into Manchester. The 1 mile, 13 chain section from Woodley Junction to Romiley was gently graded: 1-in-1100 leading to 1-in-232 giving Austerity 2-8-0 No.**90140** a breather before the gradients ahead. Comprising 20-odd wagons, the train exemplifies what might be termed a "typical" British freight (indeed, if any such thing existed). Cattle wagons, loaded and empty open-topped wagons and box vans with a guard's van at the rear to remind us that the whole ensemble was un-braked. Little of this had changed in principle since the 1840's and, certainly, nothing of it is left today. *B.K.B.Green*

Approach to Romiley Junction, n.d: A splendid view showing the layout at Romiley Junction with three lines converging. The "low-level" line or "Bredbury Curve" that we have just been looking at sweeps round on the right from Bredbury Junction. In the centre a Metro-Cammell 2-car DMU speeds away on the 1875 Manchester & Stockport (later G.C. & Midland Joint) line from here via Reddish and Belle Vue to Ashburys East Junction. Climbing away over on the right is the original line, Sheffield & Midland Joint again, that gave the Midland its first foothold in Manchester, running from here via Hyde, Guide Bridge and Fairfield to Manchester London Road. *John Fairclough*

Romiley, station exterior Spring 1962: Situated in the heart of the village which it serves, Romiley Station is unmistakable-the imposing facade and adjacent lattice-girder bridge being clear landmarks at the east end of Stockport Road. Here, again, is glimpsed the domed staircase and the signalbox amidst reminders of rail travel in what is now a bygone age of over thirty years past. Smokers were well provided for at Helliwell's little shop next to the station: "Senior Service Satisfy" says the poster over the awning, below which are advertisements for "Players" (Please), Bristol capped (sic) cigarettes and Player's Weights. Packets of 2d. Beech Nut chewing gum could be had, as well as cigarettes, from slot machines outside the shop in an age when vandalism was not prevalent. With tobacco or chewing gum purchased, passengers could survey the hoardings offering trips to Morecambe or Blackpool before buying their tickets and ascending the staircase to the platform. A Diesel Excursion to the famous Lancashire seaside resort that was noted for fresh air and fun could be had for 9/3d. Departure from here was at 10.34 a.m. *G.H.Platt*

Romiley Station, n.d: A pre-Grouping postcard view looking from the Up platform towards the junction. Romiley opened to passengers on August 5th.1862. Both sets of platform buildings had been altered, and canopies added, in 1891. At the same time, a subway was constructed with an impressive octagonal glazed tower. The original drawings show this as a very ornate pagoda-type structure, complete with a curved octagonal pinnacle and topped by a finial-not at all like the version seen here. The crossover road and the goods sidings, seen at the back of the Up platform, were abandoned in September 1965. Plainly visible is the 3-armed junction signal controlling routes via Stockport, Belle Vue and Hyde respectively.

G.K.Fox collection

Romiley Junction, Spring 1962 : Pure Midland touches, ante-dating our first view, are in evidence at Romiley showing us clearly the three-way nature of the layout here. The semaphores show the routes in a descending order of priority: left, low-level line round to Bredbury Junction; centre (pegged off), via Reddish Junction and Ashburys; right, via Hyde and Fairfield to London Road. The Midland signalbox dated from 1899; and was a replacement for the original box. Still standing today, Romiley Junction signalbox now controls the all-colour light installation as far as Ashburys East Junction, a function that came onstream in 1973. A further stage in power working came on July 28th.1980 when Romiley Junction replaced several other boxes in the area. i.e. Marple Wharf Junction, Marple and Strines.*G.H.Platt*

Leaving Romiley and its confluence of lines behind, trains head through the Cheshire countryside towards Marple. An area rich in Industrial Heritage, the environs of Marple present themselves as a by-way of tranquility, managing to survive outside the urban hustle and bustle of Metropolitan Stockport. South-east of Romiley the railway had to cross the meandering River Goyt twice in fairly close succession. Some quite spectacular civil engineering was required: two tunnels-Marple North at 99 yards and Marple South at 225 yards. Two viaducts were also required to bridge the Goyt: north of the station was Marple viaduct-918 feet long and consisting of 12 stone-built arches standing 124 feet above the river. At the south end of this impressive structure the railway had to traverse another obstacle-this time the Peak Forest Canal. The canal was crossed by means of a skew girder bridge; looking to their left, passengers see the impressive aqueduct-seven years in the building, from 1795 to 1800 and required to carry the canal over the Goyt. Into the rocky gloom of Marple North Tunnel travellers are probably unaware that the canal is literally feet above their heads! Beside the canal, at Marple Wharf Junction, so named after the short branch that once led down to the Peak ForestCanal- but abandoned c.1900-the Great Central & North Staffs. Joint line (Macclesfield, Bollington & Marple Railway) to Macclesfield Central ran off in a southerly direction. Travelling via Rose Hill and Middlewood, traffic over this line ceased in January 1970 leaving the route as a short spur to Rose Hill only.After leaving Marple Station the railway builders had literally to cut through solid rock before boring the Marple South Tunnel. Now the line clings in spectacular fashion to the rockface, some fifty feet above. Then, at Strawberry Hill, the Rover Goyt is crossed for a second time-by means of a shorter five-arched viaduct (Marple Goyt Viaduct) coupled with a single girder span that projects the railway over the river itself and on towards New Mills.

(above left). **Up I.B. Home signal from Romiley Junction, April 22nd. 1974:** Between Romiley Junction and Marple Wharf signalboxes by Wood's Bridge (No.31) was once situated a small box known as Oakwood. Housing just eight levers, Oakwood opened in 1888. Two further boxes were sited here (1892 and 1907) before closure in June 1933. Nevertheless, these semaphores remained as Up I.B. Home from Romiley Junction (previously Oakwood's Up Home) with associated splitting Distants for Marple Wharf Junction and its short branch to Rose Hill. This wooden-post signal, 30 feet high, still complete with its Midland finial, was later supplanted by a standard tubular post affair, though the splitting Distant was not retained. Re-signalling at Romiley, from July 28th.1980, saw replacement with a colour light.

(above right). **July 15th.1975:** A rear view of this splendid artefact allows study of some of the finer points of semaphore signalling, notably repeaters, guy ropes and woodwork. In the quasi-rural surroundings a Class 40 speeds by on the Down line towards Romiley. *Raymond Keeley*

Distants for Romiley Junction, Sunday, October 12th.1958: Another little signalling gem is provided by this picture of the triple splitting Distant arrangement for Romiley Junction-sited on the opposite side of the bridge in the previous picture. Perusal of the semaphores at Romiley station will show these Distants corresponding to their respective Homes. The stop signal on top of the left-hand post is another I.B. signal; formerly controlled by Oakwood, the I.B. on this side of the line was worked by the box at Marple Wharf Junction. The locomotive bursting under Wood's Bridge is Class 5 No.**44717** with an excursion working. In later years the Distant for line via Hyde was removed.
W.J.Skillern

Between Romiley and Marple Wharf, n.d: South of Wood's Bridge (No.31 in the Midland's Ambergate district bridge register) Compound 4-4-0 No. **41062** heads through the shallow cutting and along towards Marple Wharf Junction with a stopping passenger train.
W.A.Brown

Marple Viaduct c.1947: A striking view of the viaduct showing the aqueduct carrying the Peak Forest Canal over the valley in the foreground. The 4-coach train, drawn by a C13 4-4-2 tank engine, is a Manchester London Road to Macclesfield (Central) stopping train travelling over the Great Central & North Staffs. Joint line, closed south of Rose Hill in 1970. The steel girders, forming part of the viaduct, on the right-hand side take the railway over the River Goyt. The keen-eyed may be able to spot the signals at Marple Wharf Junction, pegged "off" for the Macclesfield line. *P.Ward*

Marple Viaduct n.d: Heading towards Marple Wharf, passengers receive something of an overture to the scenic delights that follow. Here, on the border of Cheshire and Derbyshire, the beautiful countryside unfolds its rich store as the line comes upon nature's obstacles and overcomes them in its march southwards. Here, in what appears as an almost aerial view, we look south towards Marple Wharf Junction as 8F 2-8-0 No.**48654** rumbles over the viaduct with a Down mixed freight comprising seventeen wagons. At the end of the viaduct, Marple Wharf Junction, together with its signalbox, can just be made out. At this point the Peak Forest Canal runs alongside the line via an aqueduct-out of sight below the trees on the right-hand side. *A.H.Bryant*

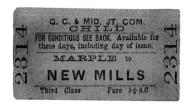

G. C. & MID. JT. COM.
CHILD
FOR CONDITIONS SEE BACK. Available for
three days, including day of issue.
MARPLE to
NEW MILLS
Third Class   Fare 3½d.0
2314   2314

Marple Viaduct, August 17th.1947: From a similar viewpoint we retrace our steps back in time to look at a vintage operation: an ex-Great Central 4-4-2 tank engine-Class C13 No.**7424** and its train-a stopping passenger containing a mixture of ex-G.C. clerestory coaches and later LNER vehicles. Though not clearly visible, the photographer has recorded that the ex-Midland Railway signals at Marple Wharf Junction (sighted on the "wrong" side of the line) are in the process of being replaced by upper-quadrant types. *P.Ward*

Marple Wharf Junction was (and still is) a very interesting location. The site of the little branch that once led down to the Peak Forest Canal, the very characteristic Midland signalbox which faced on to the sweeping curve of the erstwhile G.C. & North Staffs.

Joint line to Macclesfield conspired, together with the delightfully rural surroundings, to make something of a "picture-book" location; a modeller's delight, perhaps?

Marple Wharf Junction, May 24th.1957: Taking the route via Marple is Hughes/Fowler 0-8-0 No.**49515** with an Up freight train. The photographer is standing between the line to Macclesfield via Middlewood (high-level). Though of Midland design, the signalbox here, with its 20-lever tappet frame, was actually erected in LMS days-it opened on 11th.December 1927 replacing an earlier brick-built structure on an adjacent site. *W.A.Brown*

(left). **Marple Wharf Junction, c.1955:** Of Midland Railway Acfield-pattern, the top semaphore was Marple Wharf Junction's Down Home signal. The arm underneath was an I.B. Distant controlling the section formerly worked by Oakwood box and stretching from here to the south side of Wood's Bridge. Just about discernible in the undergrowth is the outline of the alignment of the short branch from here down to the Peak Forest Canal which had been abandoned in 1899.   *D.Ibbotson*

(right). **Marple Wharf Junction, signalbox interior, n.d:** A rare treat for signalling buffs is this view inside Marple Wharf box. No date is available, but the picture must have been taken after September 9th.1970 when Rose Hill box was closed. Despite the addition of a modern track circuited layout (which took over the functions of Rose Hill signalbox as well) and up-to-date panel, the box still retains its Midland block instruments. Notice the peculiarly forward slant of the Midland-pattern lever frame; this was due to the levers being pivoted above floor-level with the interlocking gear housed in front. Marple Wharf box became redundant on Monday, July 28th.1980 when the Romiley Junction power signalling scheme came into operation. *Author's collection*

Marple Wharf Junction, Spring 1946: J11 0-6-0, newly re-numbered **4440**, comes round the curve off the Marple line and heads towards Rose Hill with a train for Macclesfield Central.

William Lees

Marple North Tunnel, n.d: "When is a tunnel not a tunnel?" Answer: when it is described by the railway company as a "covered way." 99 yards long, Marple North tunnel took the railway just a few feet under the Peak forest Canal. It was built without ventilation shafts, but some were added in 1914. In the lovely sylvan surroundings, so typical of this section of the line, A5 4-6-2 tank No.**69823** emerges into the sunlight with an Up stopping passenger train. An interesting mixture of LNER coaching stock reveals itself: the first coach being a teak-bodied vehicle, the next four vehicles are comprised of two pairs of articulated steel-panelled coaches. *P.Ward*

Marple Station c.1900: A view looking towards Brabyns Brow, the main thoroughfare that ran past the station towards Marple Bridge, and New Mills showing the station in its almost final condition before the addition of the later platform signalbox. The black roundel on a white ground for the reverse side of the stop signals was a peculiarly Midland device; it was abandoned from around 1912. Notice the trap points at the end of the loops and the generally hemmed-in appearance of the station. Joint influence-from the M.S.& L. can be detected in the style of the lamp posts: the beautiful tulip-shaped bases of that company's ironwork is visible in both this and the accompanying picture.

G.K.Fox collection

Prior to the opening of the cut-off line via Disley Tunnel and Cheadle Heath in 1902, Marple was something of a focal point for Midland operations in and out of Manchester. The railway had arrived in 1862 when the M.S. & L's branch from Hyde was opened, via a single line, to what was known as "Compstall." Marple gradually grew in importance from 1866/67 when the Midland began to run through services from London (at first from King's Cross) to Manchester London Road. The station began life as a single-platform affair (on the Down side only). Another (Up) platform was added by 1872 and the original platform was lengthened to around 530 feet. Goods facilities and bay platforms had been added by 1875 when the station was rebuilt. Both platforms were lengthened and widened and the Down platform was provided with a splendid glass and iron canopy 350 feet long. The Up platform was provided with a loop giving the station four platform faces in all. Water columns and a 45 ft. turntable gave rudimentary engine servicing facilities. Today's comparatively sparse traffic on this section of the line gives the modern observer little clue as to what operations of yesteryear were like here. Marple was considered important enough in the 1870s for no less than six Pullman trains to call; no less than 46 Midland trains per day paid a call at this time (the late 1870s.) Vast quantities of freight would have rolled through Marple in the latter part of the nineteenth century, an era we tend to regard as the heyday of the railway system.

In particular, huge amounts of coal were required to fire the various industries in Lancashire and much of this would have come via the Midland route. Still more freight traffic came onstream after the Midland company opened the Ancoats goods depot, almost in the heart of Manchester, in 1870. Further passenger traffic arrived in 1894 when the Midland Railway's Dore and Chinley line (popularly known as "The Hope Valley Line") opened for traffic. By this time Marple was literally bursting at the seams and expansion, though not impossible, would have been extremely difficult. The station was literally hemmed in by its surroundings. It was now towards Chinley that the Midland looked for its expansion of through and connecting services to and from Manchester. Here, a grand new station with five main line platforms plus a bay for the new line to Sheffield. Four tracks were provided north of Chinley and a large complex of sidings for the interchange of trans-Pennine freight was built at Gowholes, just south of New Mills. At New Mills itself the junction between the old line via Marple and Stockport and the new line through Disley Tunnel was established. Marple, though not entirely eclipsed, now became something of a backwater. With its plans to capture for itself a major slice of the north-west passenger and freight market complete, the Midland was able to face the twentieth century with confidence.

Marple Station, 1957: A modern view, one that makes an interesting comparison with the previous shot. Taken from more or less the same angle, we see Marple some half a century later. In the Down through platform is a A5 4-6-2 tank No.**69815** with the 1.30 p.m. Hayfield to Manchester train. Alongside in the bay platform, not quite so prominent, is C14 4-4-2 tank No.67448 with the 2.18 p.m. Marple to Manchester local. Though outside the scope of this book, passenger services to Hayfield finished on January 5th.1970. The platform signalbox was inaugurated on March 12th.1905 at which time two other boxes-Marple Station and Marple North were taken out of use. As at Marple Wharf Junction, this signalbox, too, was abolished under the Romiley-New Mills re-signaling scheme in July 1980.   *W.A.Brown*

Marple Signalbox, 1930: A glimpse inside the box at Marple which housed a 33-lever Midland tumbler frame. The signalman was Walter Morris but, sadly, we know nothing about him. Walter's appearance is typical of that of so many uniformed staff of the bygone railway era: collar and tie, buttoned waistcoat, watch chain and a general business-like appearance. Midland-pattern block instruments complete the picture.   *G.H.Platt*

Marple Station, May 13th.1968: One in a series of official views taken at Marple-probably to record the dilapidated state of the platform canopies. The station architecture here was, indeed, splendid; but the lavish nature of the provision which was reflected in the style and sheer quantity of it all made modern maintenance a nightmare. With the drastic reduction in services something of a simpler, easier to maintain building fabric had to be considered. In consequence, alterations and rebuilding were deemed necessary. In December 1963 the Down loop platform and associated trackwork were taken out of use; the Up side followed, likewise, in October 1964. Beginning in January 1970 the station itself was rebuilt. All the existing station buildings, including the covered footbridge that ran from Brabyns Brow-just visible in the right of the picture-were demolished. The platforms were both shortened and raised in height-by 9". Of the original 1875 structure, only the footbridge-glimpsed beyond the partly-ruined canopy was considered sound enough to be retained. The goods yard was closed on October 5th.1964 and, very sensibly, turned into a car park. The goods shed was demolished at the same time by the Divisional Engineer (Nottingham). Platform notices are worth a mention: one hoarding announces new booking arrangements for services on the Piccadilly-Hayfield line with effect from March 24th.1968. An adjacent poster shows 49 trains departing from Marple at the time the picture was taken.

Marple (Down platform canopies and buildings), May 13th.1968: The buildings and low-level canopy within our immediate focus date from the station's opening in 1865. The 1875 canopy, complete with LMR maroon totem, runs along at a higher level. The awning supports for this later structure carried integrally-cast roundels bearing the intertwined initials "S&M" (Sheffield and Midland). Some of these are believed to have survived in private hands after demolition. Those buildings seen here housed the various station offices. Set just to the right is the station house, whilst adjacent to the later canopy is a porter's room and store.

Marple, (view of Up platform and footbridge) May 13th.1968: Bridge 26A was the impressive covered footbridge leading from Brabyn's Brow directly down onto to the Up platform. Seen here in its last years, the structure was a legacy from the heyday of the railway system in this country when passenger provision thrived on a grand scale.

Marple, (inside of covered footbridge) May 13th.1968: A total span of 126 feet was provided by bridge 26A-an impressive structure and one that had been a focal point at Marple since its erection in 1875. Here we look towards the Up platform, noticing that gas-as in the booking office-is the source of illumination. Who, one wonders, was Keith Tomlinson of Gorton?!

Marple Station, (booking office interior) May 13th.1968: Hardly changed in almost a hundred years, this was the inside of Marple's booking office; Mr.Peter McAnulty was the Stationmaster at the time this picture was taken. Familiar to anyone versed in the operation of such a place are the racks with their myriads of different tickets, neat piles of cash and notices held together with the ubiquitous bulldog clips. Over the wooden cupboard are the rate books for parcels and freight, side by side with such things as the legendary Railway Clearing House book of stations showing everywhere from Abbey to Ystradowen. At night the booking office would take on an almost eerie glow as the gently hissing gas mantles cast their yellow light over the dark brown of the ageing woodwork and feet sounded and squeaked upon the bare boards to greet the traveller at the ticket window. All from a bygone age and long vanished now.

All pictures, British Railways

Marple, April 15th.1966: The dilapidations of the station canopy are evident as the clock reaches twenty-two minutes past two, thank you Keith!, to witness the arrival of Class 5 No.**45404** with an Up 3-coach stopping train bound, possibly, for Sheffield via the Hope Valley. Notice the LNER-style shed name painted on the buffer beam in white lettering. Something of junior contemporary male fashion can be seen amongst the train spotters.   *A.K.Rathbone*

Marple South Tunnel c.1955: About a quarter of a mile from Marple station trains were required to penetrate nature's obstacles, again via a tunnel. Marple South Tunnel had been constructed about (sic) 1861 and was 224 yards long. It was shortened by 45 yards and widened at the north end between 1874 and 1875. No ventilation shafts had been provided when the tunnel was built; a situation remedied in 1914.

D.Ibbotson

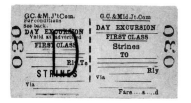

Between Marple and Strines n.d: Once over Goyt Cliff Viaduct the line, heading now towards Strines and New Mills, climbs at 1-in-100. Strawberry Hill, Collier's Farm, Green Clough, Brook Bottom; such peculiarly English-sounding names abound where the railway rubs shoulders with the boundary between Cheshire and Derbyshire on its route south to Chinley. Here, the lovely rural surroundings speak for themselves as Class 5 No.**44895** ruffles the calm of a summer day heading for Strines with a four coach stopping train.*A.K.Rathbone*

Marple, Goyt Viaduct c.1956: Emerging from the gloom of Marple South Tunnel, trains have to travel just under three-quarters of a mile to reach the second of Marple's viaducts. This, smaller, one is known locally as Marple Goyt Viaduct, but the Midland bridge register refers to it as "Goyt Cliff Viaduct." Whatever the precise name it is an impressive structure, crossing both the River Goyt and its associated valley-an area which has become famous for its "Roman Lakes." Just about to cross the river section of the viaduct is an unidentified 8F 2-8-0 heading towards Romiley with a loaded coal train. The octagonal-shaped house below the arches is believed to have been built c.1801. It was occupied by the lock keeper whose job it would have been to control the flow of water to the main reservoir of nearby Mellor Mill. *P.Ward*

Marple, Goyt Viaduct n.d: A second look at this attractive structure, again with an 8F, and underlining just how much freight once travelled this route. The train has cleared the River Goyt and is just about to regain land again before heading towards Strines. Let us complete our look at Marple's viaducts by quoting from the Midland Railway bridge register. This is the entry for the Goyt Cliff viaduct: "Stone abutments, wings and piers. Over land, etc.; stone parapets, and 2ft.9ins. arches; 5 spans, 45ft. 0 ins. each. Over River Goyt: 2 W.I. (wrought iron) main deck girders, with bracing, cross girders, with centre steel lattice distributing girder., 4 ins. timber floor, W.I. lattice parapets; span, 82ft. 0 ins. Over land etc.; stone parapets, and 2 ft. 9ins. arches; 2 spans, 45 ft. 0 ins. each; total, 8 spans; length, 161 yards. Constructed about 1861; river span, bracing and centre girder, added, 1893." (The section over the river was re-decked in 1973). A small signalbox once stood by Goyt Viaduct. Housing a six-lever tumbler frame it had been erected in 1904; it was taken out of use at the same time as Oakwood and its functions were retained as an I.B. worked by Marple station box (Up line) and Strines (Down line). *A.K.Rathbone*

Strines, March 19th.1949: Approaching Strines station the ascending gradient continued at 1-in-100, easing slightly to 1-in-114 before a brief stretch of level line near milepost 174. Some 27 wooden-bodied wagons are giving 4F No.**4205** a breathless few minutes as it clears Green Clough bridge and approaches Strines station on its way south towards New Mills. *J.D.Darby*

Strines Station n.d: Strines, Hayfield, New Mills, Chinley-these are all names forever associated with hiking and rambling in the North-West. A glorious summer day is in the heaven and wild flowers are in abundance as we pause outside Strines station to watch C14 No.**67448** pulling away with a train from Hayfield to Manchester London Road. *W.A.Brown*

Strines Station May 28th.1953: The many and varied architectural styles of the pre-Grouping companies, together with a myriad of details in the shape and form of such things as name boards and platform furniture brought tremendous individuality to the one-time railway scene. Sadly, much of this has now gone as a much-critiscised railway system struggles to come to terms with its finances. It is as a result of these strictures that stations such as Strines have become almost anonymous. With buildings demolished, lamp posts removed and staff gone, many British railway stations, indeed, those lucky enough to have survived at all!, live on at only a basic functional level. All of such one-time character is manifest here at Strines as "Crab" 2-6-0 No.**42934** breezes through with train C903-empty stock from an excursion to Belle Vue, Manchester.

B.K.B.Green

Strines Station n.d: This was the Up platform waiting shelter at Strines and was a later addition-the line was originally single from New Mills and only buildings on the Down side were provided at first. With its Pagoda-style roof, the little building, though of Derby design, is vaguely reminiscent of structures built by a certain company who had considerable branch line interests in Devon and Cornwall. Only the Midland Railway company's gas lamp posts tell us this is territory nearer to home. No doubt reduced staffing levels are responsible for the disappearance of the neat and trim little garden. An LMR maroon enamelled sign board has replaced the earlier wooden one and the lamp posts have lost their ornate tapered and capped tops. Today, with all the buildings gone, Strines is only identifiable by the drab black-on-white nameboards. The corporate image rules! *G.K.Fox*

Strines, April 23rd.1952: Then an almost new engine, B.R. Standard Class 5 No.**73015** runs into Strines with the 1.05 p.m. Derby to Manchester Central stopping train. Strines signalbox was built to a standard Midland Railway period II design and dated from November 19th.1893. Housing 12 levers in a tumbler-pattern frame (dating from 1904)it replaced an earlier box, a scenario that should now be fairly familiar to readers of this this little line history. The small goods yard, seen running off to the right of the picture, had only two sidings: one was for coal traffic whilst the other serviced the needs of a local company-the Strines Calico Print Works; this second siding was provided with a goods shed. The yard closed on August 12th.1963. *B.K.B.Green*

Leaving Strines, March 19th.1949: The Up Starter is pegged "off" as 8F No.**48349** runs slowly past at the head of a train of empty wagons. Comprised of the wooden-bodied, former P.O. type of wagon, the formation of freight trains in this era presented a rather sort of ragged outline compared to later years when the 16-ton all-steel B.R. standard mineral types came on the scene. *J.D.Darby*

Hague Bar n.d: Roughly half-way between Strines and New Mills is the hamlet of Hague Bar nestling on the north-eastern side of the Sett Valley. With a loaded ballast train, thirteen wagons plus two brake vans, Austerity 2-8-0 No.**90202** clears Hague Bar bridge and runs along the Up line towards New Mills.   *A.H.Bryant*

Hague Bar n.d: "The railway in the Derbyshire landscape" is how I would describe this view. Here we see the whole panorama from Hague Bar to New Mills as a pair of Derby Lightweight DMU sets pick up speed and make for Strines. New Mills is in the background, Hague Bar above, in this splendid scene. Just behind the train are the splitting Distant signals for New Mills: left for the Hayfield branch via Birch Vale; right for the main line via New Mills Goods to New Mills South Junction.   *A.H.Bryant*

New Mills

The Derbyshire town of New Mills, its stone-built properties taking shelter away from the ever-busy A6 road, has the luxury of two railway stations to serve its needs. Newtown Station, at the south end of the town just near the A6, is served by the Manchester-Buxton line trains; an all-Sprinter service now but surviving as part of the Regional Railways network, having doughtily fought off the scalpel of one, Dr.Beeching. On the opposite side of the valley, just off Marple Road, is New Mills Central; opened on July 1st.1865, the name was changed from plain "New Mills" on August 25th.1952. New Mills was the junction for the three mile branch to Hayfield. With one intermediate station only-at Birch Vale-the Hayfield branch closed to passengers on January 5th.1970, the same day as the Rose Hill to Macclesfield line. As with all the rest of the Midland's routes to Manchester as far as Heaton Mersey, the Hayfield branch was also a piece of joint territory-Sheffield & Midland Joint). From New Mills Junction-just east of the station, however, the Midland were their own masters.

New Mills, (looking to Strines) n.d: The Derbyshire hills are in evidence as we look from New Mills westwards towards Strines. To the right of the sidings, by the Up line, is what appears to be a miniature signalbox. This rather curious-looking structure was in fact a platelayers' cabin, the ground at the back of the sidings being designated "permanent way storage ground." Notice the combination of Up and Down stop signals on a common post-a not untypical Midland practice, Q.V. West Didsbury. *G.H.Platt*

(above). **New Mills, Up Home and Down Starting signals:** A close-up picture of the signals seen in the previous view. The splitting Home signals relate to the Hayfield branch and main line respectively: left for the branch, right for Up main. Sitting squatly below is the Down Starting signal. *D.Ibbotson*

New Mills Station, n.d: A reproduction from an old postcard looking towards New Mills Junction, Buxworth and Chinley. Beyond the footbridge can be seen the mouth of one of the two tunnels driven through the rock at the east end of the station. One tunnel, 242 yards long, took the line through to Hayfield; the other, at 123 yards, took the railway on towards New Mills Goods and New Mills South Junction. The postcard carries the heading "New Mills East"-a misnomer as the suffix was never carried by the station, only the goods yard. *Lens of Sutton*

New Mills Central. c.1965. This mid summer scene shows the station in a view south from the Down platform, looking towards Chinley. The lack of custom perhaps indicates that the signal is "off" for the passage of a freight train, although quite frequently passengers would emerge at the last moment from the shelter. The station was still served by trains on the Manchester Piccadilly to Hayfield service, some 20 Up and 21 Down during the week, not bad for something under threat. Together with the "turn-backs" and Sheffield to Derby workings, New Mills had upwards of seventy trains stopping during each weekday.   *D.Ibbotson.*

New Mills Station, (Up platform) c.1965: Long before closure of the Woodhead line to Sheffield in July 1981, Manchester-Sheffield passenger traffic was being concentrated on the Midland's Hope Valley line. Thus, after closure of Central Station, along with the South District line in 1969, Trains between the two cities were using a rather curious mixture of routes: the "old" route south to London via Ashburys, Belle Vue and Romiley-abandoned when the South District became available in 1877, and the "new" line from Chinley to Dore and Totley-opened in 1894. After the opening of the Hazel Grove Chord in May, 1986, trains from Piccadilly could take an entirely new route to Sheffield: using the LNWR line to Stockport and the Buxton branch to just beyond Hazel Grove, the east-bound traffic could use the newly-laid line to gain the 1902 Midland line, travel via Disley Tunnel and once more gain the Hope Valley route at Chinley North Junction. Here at New Mills Class 31 No.**D5848**, in two-tone green livery, pays a call with an Up Sheffield working. 31s were favourites for a long time on these services and their use continued until well after the Hazel Grove Chord opened; they were eventually replaced by the ubiquitous "Sprinters." D5848 met an early demise when, as 31 314 it was withdrawn (on September 10th.1982) after a collision at Lindsey Oil Refinery on July 30th.1982 with 56 004   *A.H.Bryant*

New Mills Station, June 2nd.1955: Here we look down from Station Road, over the footbridge, on to the Down platform and buildings and over towards Strines. The "Central" tag firmly marks this station out from its ex-LNWR neighbour over at Newtown, something reinforced by the Midland-pattern lamps and signals. As at Strines and Marple these buildings, together with the Down platform, comprised the original station provision here-one single track sufficing when the railway opened in 1865. Nearest the camera is the booking office and hall with ladies and gents waiting rooms in between together with the "usual offices." At the far end was sited the Stationmaster's house. A hoarding by the station entrance advertises an excursion to Blackpool for 13/- (65p).

H.B.Priestley

New Mills Central. c.1965. View south from the Up platform showing the station signal box tucked away behind the bridge carrying Station Road. The structure dated from 1908, having replaced the original of 1861. The footbridge, numbered 14A, reflected a design favoured by the Midland Railway at the time of construction in 1903. It replaced an earlier wooden type of 1887.

D. Ibbotson.

New Mills Central. c.1965. Another view south this time from the parapet of Back Union Road above the 123 yard long New Mills Tunnel. The parapet walls of the viaduct over the River Kinder extend out in the foreground. The stone overbridge carries Hyde Bank Road over the railway, overlooked at this point by the aptly named 'Midland Terrace' displaying a stone tablet dated 1903.

D. Ibbotson.

New Mills Station, tunnel entrances: An interesting view showing the two tunnel mouths: left taking the branch to Hayfield and right the line towards New Mills South Junction. Though the Hayfield line has long been lifted, Hayfield tunnel survives as a means of reversing for DMUs that terminate here before returning to Manchester. Of particular note is the splendid Midland-pattern three-armed semaphore. Left and right are Starters: for the Hayfield branch and main line respectively; beneath are appropriate Distants: left for New Mills tunnel End box (a 10-lever affair between the Tunnel here and Birch Vale-closed on January 4th.1970) and right for New Mills Goods Junction. The centre Distant arm is for the New Mills Up Goods loop. *R.E.Gee*

New Mills, (east end of main line tunnel) 1933: The stone-built terraces of New Mills, perched high above the railway, form a backcloth to this scene as we watch LMS Compound No.**1055** pull away from the tunnel mouth with an Up stopping train. Immediately beyond the tunnel is the Sett viaduct: described in the bridge register as New Mills Viaduct, two of the four spans are just visible under the train. Comprising four arches, and of sixty yards length, the structure spans the Sett Valley and the River Kinder-a name forever associated with the Peak District. *E.R.Morten.*

New Mills Goods Junction n.d: A view of New Mills Goods Junction, looking towards New Mills South Junction. Situated just twenty-three chains east of New Mills Junction, where the Hayfield line parted company with the main line, this was New Mills Goods. The signalbox, to Midland period III design, had been provided as a replacement as recently as December 1928. Housing 35 levers, 26 operational, 9 spares, the box was situated on the Up side of the line. Goods facilities at New Mills (the depot had been re-named "New Mills East Goods Depot" in 1924) lay on the Down side of the line with a goods loop, some 50 chains long, lying alongside the Up line-on the left of our view here. The yard, seen off to the right, dated from 1872 and wagon capacity was given as 280 on the Midland's track diagrams. An example of the huge volume of freight carried in these parts can be gleaned from official statistics at the PRO, Kew. In 1901 no less than 52,245 tons of coal, coke and limestone were handled at New Mills. Two years later general freight traffic peaked at 38,990 tons overall. The two goods sheds provided here were shown on fire insurance plans as holding hemp, grain, waste, flour and general merchandise. New Mills Goods box was closed on September 9th.1968; just for the record it was demolished for the sum of £148.10/-. Goods traffic was then transferred to Stockport Edgeley although the yard itself was not closed, but was retained to serve Engineers' traffic in the form of Mermaid (ballast) wagons until accommodation could be found for them at Peak Forest. Final closure was effected on June 4th.1969.*G.H.Platt*

New Mills East, March 14th.1953: Atmospheric pollution on a grand scale is practised by Austerity 2-8-0 No.**90546** as it clears New Mills Goods and heads towards New Mills South Junction with a mixed freight, an all-out effort by the looks of things. The picture gives some idea of the track layout here: New Mills goods sidings are off to the left of the picture; No.90546 is travelling along the Up line-Up Slow line from New Mills South towards Gowhole. Beyond the train can just be glimpsed the Up Goods line-a loop-52 chains (just over half a mile) long between here and New Mills South Junction.   *T.Lewis*